PRESENTING

Norma Klein

TUSAS 538

Twayne's United States Authors Series
Young Adult Authors

Patricia J. Campbell, General Editor

The Young Adult Authors books seek to
meet the need for critical studies of fiction
for young adults. Each volume examines
the life and work of one author, helping
both teachers and readers of young adult
literature to understand better the writers
they have read with such pleasure
and fascination.

PRESENTING

Norma Klein

Allene Stuart Phy

Twayne Publishers • Boston
A Division of G. K. Hall & Co.

Presenting Norma Klein
Allene Stuart Phy

© 1988 by G. K. Hall & Co.
All rights reserved.
Published by Twayne Publishers
A Division of G. K. Hall & Co.
70 Lincoln Street
Boston, Massachusetts 02111

Photographs kindly provided by Norma Klein.

Copyediting supervised by Barbara Sutton.
Book design by Marne Sultz.
Book production by Janet Zietowski.

Typeset in 10/13 pt. Century Schoolbook
by Modern Graphics, Inc., Weymouth, Massachusetts

Printed on permanent/durable acid-free paper
and bound in the United States of America

Library of Congress Cataloging in Publication Data

Phy, Allene Stuart.
 Presenting Norma Klein / Allene Stuart Phy.
  p. cm. — (Twayne's United States authors series ; TUSAS
 538. Young adult authors)
  Bibliography: p.
  Includes index.
  ISBN 0–8057–8205–2 (alk. paper)
  1. Klein, Norma, 1938– —Criticism and interpretation. 2. Young adult fiction, American—History and criticism. I. Title. II. Series: Twayne's United
States authors series ; TUSAS 538. III. Series: Twayne's United States authors series. Young adult authors.
PS3561.L35Z8 1988
813′.54—dc19   88-514
                                                          CIP

*To the memory of Warren Titus,
honored mentor and colleague,
who completed a distinguished career
by teaching juvenile and young adult literature.*

Contents

Preface

Norma Klein, like Stephen King or Agatha Christie, is a member of a small fraternity of "brand-name" authors. The King, Christie, or Klein label guarantees a product of flair and liveliness, not suited to every taste but widely sought. One problem with becoming a brand-name author, however, is that a writer thereby becomes typecast. To most of the reading public, Klein is simply considered a young adult author.

Though best known for her teenage fiction, Klein has also written seven children's books, which are still widely available and frequently discussed. Many of her admirers are unaware that she is the author of more than a dozen books for adults as well, including two collections of short stories of superb quality. At her best, Klein is one of the finest writers in the young adult field, with at least two classics, *Angel Face* and *Hiding,* and two highly innovative contributions, *Mom, the Wolf Man, and Me* and *Going Backwards,* to her credit. Her short fiction, somewhat obscured in two improperly reviewed anthologies, *Sextet* and *Love and Other Euphemisms,* ranks with the best now being written.

The juvenile and young adult literary establishment still does not know quite what to make of Klein. Librarians, teachers, and parents are not always sure they like or trust her as a guide for youth. The belief is still widespread that a writer of teenage fiction should serve a cautionary, instructive function, should be a sort of Ann Landers or "Miss Manners." Klein often appears too hedonistic a mentor, and her very popularity may sometimes make her suspect. Though she is widely read by the young and cherished by every paperback book dealer, she is not the sort of writer who wins awards from the American Library Association. Despite her personal charm and lively manner of speaking, she is not very frequently invited to address education groups. She is no television talk-show personality, like Judy Blume, whom many people assume to be rival but who is actually her friend.

Though Klein has thousands of readers in what many New Yorkers think of as the hinterland—the rest of the country—her almost constant advocacy of New York City has alienated some serious adult readers, who find in her writing an urban provincialism. They resent what they regard as Klein's casual dismissal of the rest of the country, particularly when she permits a fictional character to express the opinion that a young person sent to a state university in Louisiana, for example, faces a fate like unto exile or disgrace. There is much anti–New York sentiment abroad in the land, and Klein has had a considerable amount of it focused on her.

In the last decade a substantial portion of serious juvenile fiction has moved from genteel realism into a modified form of literary naturalism. The ghetto and its problems and the plight of oppressed ethnic minorities, the poor, and the handicapped have all been celebrated in books that often proclaim their social consciousness in blaring tones. Norma Klein has not much participated in this trendy preaching. She has remained a recorder of bourgeois mores and the values of her characters have been largely those of the Jewish upper-middle class. Many patrons of juvenile fiction feel her sympathies have consequently been too limited, her protagonists have too consistently been budding Portnoys and Jewish-American princesses.

Yet the major problem librarians and teachers have had with Klein is the special sort of controversy she habitually generates. As taboos have seemed, however slowly, to be disappearing in young adult writing, Klein has managed to march a few paces ahead of other iconoclasts. She has—with considerably more literary finesse and even more boldness than Judy Blume—constantly explored sexuality. In fiction designed for those hardly out of nursery school themselves, she has allowed kindergarten girls to speculate openly on the anatomies of their brothers. In her books, young children have sometimes entered their parents' bedrooms at inopportune moments, and teenagers have had sexual encounters with growing frequency and without remorse. Some of her young people have come to pleasant terms with gay uncles or even lesbian mothers.

Klein's fictional teenagers are not beyond uttering an expletive now and then, or even a four-letter verb. In one of her latest young adult books, Klein has tackled a taboo even stronger in the genre than sex: euthanasia. In her practice and eloquently in her personal voice, she has struggled against editors and school boards for freedom of the pen.

Norma Klein is a woman with a mission, perhaps with several missions. She wants good books to be written for young people, books that will be evaluated with the same seriousness accorded to adult writing. She also wants the freedom for herself and other writers in the field to represent life as they see it. She seeks the opportunity, as well, to battle what she views as the two chief barriers to the fulfillment of youthful promise: sexual repression and male chauvinism.

Though Klein may sometimes sacrifice literary values to her causes, and though her stridency may tire some readers, her courage cannot but be admired, even if a reader disagrees with her priorities or rejects some of her premises. While there is justification for some of the criticism she has received, both her critics and her advocates have frequently been narrow in their discernments. Klein is often liked or disliked for reasons that have little to do with literary merit. She is admired for her boldness and her advocacy of liberal ideas, or she is condemned for the same reasons.

Klein, however, is a woman of letters even more than she is the chronicler of sexual emancipation or women's liberation. (Changing social attitudes and practices may quickly date seemingly bold proclamations on these issues, and perhaps already have done so.) She deserves literary consideration before any other form of attention. Because her first novel, *Mom, the Wolf Man and Me,* remains one of her best, it is easy to forget that she is a constantly developing and expanding writer, in midcareer. When she has taken new directions in her novels—writing from the point of view of a young male or choosing protagonists from the

PRESENTING NORMA KLEIN

lower class of a small town—she has usually been successful. While the final word cannot yet be pronounced on Klein the writer, because her own final words are far from written, her career is now sufficiently established that an evaluation of the midpoint achievement is not out of order.

For this study I have reread all Klein's published fiction (a pleasurable task), whether written for children, young adults, or adults. I have also been able to examine one novel in manuscript form. Additional information has been provided by Klein's essays, which have appeared in a number of journals, and by the few brief scholarly discussions of her work that have already been published. I have attempted to track down all major reviews of her books. A further constant source of tantalizing opinion on Klein has been conversation with many readers, teachers, librarians, and book dealers. I have discovered that all these people have strong feelings about her and, frequently, piquant insights.

Norma Klein, the most helpful and accessible of authors, has been especially generous with her time. Information otherwise unattributed in this book came directly from interviews or correspondence with her. She took time from her busy writing schedule to check the biographical chapter for accuracy. The critical opinions expressed in this book, except those quoted from other scholars, are my own and have not been reviewed or approved by Klein.

I am also especially indebted to Professor Mark West of the University of North Carolina at Charlotte for sharing with me the witty and informative tapes of his own interview with Klein. Parts of this interview have been published in the *New York Times Book Review.*

Twayne Publishers and editors Ron Brown and Patricia J. Campbell are to be commended for choosing to devote one of the early volumes in this series to this popular and significant writer, even though she is not a particular favorite of the juvenile and young adult literary establishment. Athenaide Dallett is an especially perceptive and helpful editor, one of the best I have ever worked with.

I would also like to thank my dear husband, Professor Frederick

Preface

B. Olsen, an author and literary critic, for his valuable insights and helpful analyses of the psychology of Klein's fictional characters.

We will all be pleased if this book opens further discussion of this bold and innovative writer, and of her books, which are so intriguingly a mirror of their times.

Allene Stuart Phy

Alabama State University

Chronology

PRESENTING NORMA KLEIN

1975 *What It's All About,* for older children; *Blue Trees, Red Sky,* for children; *Sunshine,* a novel based on a television production written by Carol Sobieski; and *The Sunshine Years,* its sequel.

1976 *Girls Turn Wives,* for adults, and *Hiding,* for young adults.

1977 *It's OK If You Don't Love Me,* published on the adult lists; *Sunshine Christmas,* the last of the Sunshine novelizations; father, Dr. Emanuel Klein, dies.

1978 *Love is One of the Choices,* on the adult lists; *Tomboy,* sequel to *Confessions of an Only Child,* for children.

1979 *French Postcards,* a novel from the film, and *Visiting Pamela,* the last of the children's books.

1980 *Breaking Up,* for young adults, and *A Honey of a Chimp,* for older children.

1981 *Domestic Arrangements,* on the adult lists, and *Robbie and the Leap Year Blues,* for older children.

1982 *Wives and Other Women,* for adults, and *The Queen of the What Ifs,* for young adults.

1983 *Sextet in A Minor,* the second short story collection; *The Swap,* on the adult lists, *Beginner's Love* and *Bizou,* for young adults; *Baryshnikov's Nutcracker,* a fictional adaptation from the ballet.

1984 *Lovers,* for adults; *Angel Face* and *Snapshots,* for young adults.

1985 *Give and Take,* published on adult lists; *The Cheerleader* and *Family Secrets,* for young adults.

1986 *Going Backwards,* for young adults.

1987 *American Dreams,* for adults, and *Older Men,* for young adults.

1. Life and Writings: The Feminist Homebody at Work

Norma Klein is a small, attractive woman who would have been described in pre–women's liberation days as "a pretty brunette lady who writes books." She likes to characterize herself as a middle-aged feminist who is also deeply involved in family life. Though she has been happily married for over two decades, she chooses to be known by her maiden name. By this she bears witness to her strong conviction that a woman should be her own person and not merely a shadow of her husband. Also, by making this patronymic famous, she honors her father, an extraordinary man who encouraged her writing from the beginning and whose personality in several ways continues to dominate her creative imagination.

A thoroughgoing New Yorker, Norma Klein was born in that city on 13 May 1938, the first child and only daughter of Emanuel and Sadie Frankel Klein.[1] Her father, who came to the United States from Poland at the age of five, was the son of a Talmudic scholar whom Norma remembers as a quiet man usually found reading the Yiddish newspaper. Her grandfather meticulously observed the laws of his Jewish faith, and the entire family kept Passover as long as he lived. After his death, the family no longer observed Jewish ceremonies. Norma's paternal grandmother, on the other hand, had shown little interest in Judaism from the

1

beginning, and she had been less than enthusiastic about her professionally arranged marriage. Instead, she had lavished her affection on her son Emanuel. An ambitious and energetic woman, she learned the art of the masseuse—before the notorious massage parlors defamed that honorable trade—and started spending winters in Florida, where she attended the prosperous matrons vacationing there. A clever boy who always accompanied his mother, Emanuel Klein occupied himself by tutoring the sons of her clients, who all hoped to qualify for fine eastern schools. Though the family was never well off, its members valued learning, worked hard, and were ambitious. With his mother's constant encouragement, Emanuel attended Cornell, then medical school, and eventually became a psychoanalyst.

Emanuel Klein was the center of his daughter's life while she was growing up. She admits being attached to him with what Mary Godwin Shelley, an earlier writer infatuated with a strong paternal figure, called "an extravagant and romantic passion." Though he was philosophically a pessimistic man, who initially resisted having children because he felt the state of the world was too grim (it was the period of the Nazi rise to power in Europe), he adored Norma from the moment of her birth, replicating with her, in reverse, the relationship he had experienced with his own mother. He imbued her with the confidence that she could accomplish anything. It is probably her father's early faith in her that enables her even today to persevere when feeling discouraged or depressed at rejections or bad reviews.

Emanuel was a complex man who did not relate as well to his son, Victor, born sixteen months after Norma, or to his wife, Sadie. Though he was a talented Freudian analyst, he seems, paradoxically, to have been oblivious of the implications of his excessive affection for his daughter and the consequences it might well have had on her later life. He certainly did nothing to discourage her doting affection. And she did adore him, finding him zany, outspoken, and fun, despite his cynicism about the world and human nature. She loved evenings out with him, in picturesque ethnic restaurants and at the opera or ballet. With equal readiness, she accepted his gifts of jewelry, furs, and money. Of course, there was nothing openly sexual in the relationship, for Emanuel Klein was a responsible man brought up with Old World Jewish standards of integrity. Yet Norma was, even as a girl, aware that their attachment was a genuine source of conflict within the family, since the favoritism was, understandably, resented by both her brother and mother.

After she married, she admits to having felt slightly bigamous, loving her husband and father almost equally. Emanuel continued to encourage her writing ambitions, providing regular sums of money that enabled her to employ domestic help, thus freeing her to write. Norma acknowledges today that in many important ways she wrote to please her father. His desire for grandchildren was also critical in her own decision to have children.

So deeply dependent was she on him personally and professionally that she experienced what she calls a "breakdown" after his death in 1977. For a year she could scarcely bring herself to write, and she even contemplated other careers. What use was literary acclaim, she wondered, if her father was no longer able to savor it with her. Though Klein does not believe in God and was not brought up to be religious, she remembers, significantly, that as a child she regarded her father as a quasi-deity. When he died there was not only the grief of losing a beloved companion; there was the further shock of discovering that he was not omnipotent.

Only now is she beginning to come to terms, through the catharsis of writing, with her complicated and intense relationship with her father. Armed with considerable psychological sophistication, she is now reflecting on the deeper meanings of what may accurately be called "a fixation." Norma Klein had already written factually about her feelings for her father and discussed them movingly in interviews, even before she was able to deal with them through her most recent fiction, *Going Backwards* and *Older Men.*

After Emanuel Klein's death, she made an especially startling discovery, which, had it become general knowledge during his life, would certainly have cost him his medical license and probably opened him to criminal prosecution as well. For as long as he could, Emanuel lovingly cared for his own mother in her last illness, as she was lapsing into incoherence with Alzheimer's disease. When he and his family could no longer cope with her problems, he still could not bring himself to commit her to an institution. Instead, he used his physician's knowledge and access to drugs to end her life discreetly and painlessly with a calculated dose of medication. Whatever guilt he may have carried to his deathbed (and *Going Backwards* implies that there was plenty), he had, nevertheless, made a heroic and merciful gesture, even though he was, again, playing God.

Norma Klein's mother, Sadie Frankel, came from a poor Jewish family that, unlike Emanuel's kin, did not promote learning. She grew up in Weekauken, New Jersey, the neglected youngest of seven children, in a family that included retarded brothers, pregnant and abandoned sisters, and suicide victims. Her own mother had been vehemently opposed to any of her children marrying outside the Jewish faith. As a result, several of Sadie's brothers never married. Shy and tentative in youth, Sadie was a handsome woman who always reminded her daughter of photographs of Virginia Woolf. Though her marriage to a professional man gave her upper-middle-class status, she remained melancholy and sensitive, eager to complete the education cut short in her teenage years by lack of financial support.

After living in the shadow of a successful and strong-willed husband for many years, Sadie Klein came into her own as a widow. Today she is far from anyone's stereotype of "an elderly lady." After attending college classes off and on for years, she received a B.A. in 1983, at the age of seventy-seven. She now travels, is socially active, remains intellectually inquiring, plays excellent tennis, and enjoys her children and grandchildren.

It is clear that Norma Klein learned much from her talented parents. A look at their photographs reveals a strong physical resemblance; she has inherited many of the lovely features of Sadie as well as the smile and dancing eyes of Emanuel.

The third member of the immediate family, who remains an important person in Norma Klein's life, is her brother, Victor. As children they were engaged in a constant competition that Norma, the elder and preferred child, usually won. She was the child who did well in school, while Victor was an erratic student. It was she who pleased her parents, with talents that were much admired and discussed in the family. Victor claimed fewer obvious achievements about which they could boast. Nevertheless, without other brothers and sisters and because of their closeness in age, Norma and her brother were friends. With the sibling rivalry now long past, Victor, who is a social worker in New York City, is in telephone contact with his sister several times a week. He married for the first time at the age of forty-five and is now a father. Though he does not read his sister's fiction—at least not officially—and appears indifferent to her celebrity, he is a personal friend, as well as a beloved brother.

Norma was identified as an intellectual from early childhood by her doting parents and teachers. She was sent to private, progressive schools from the age of three and graduated from Elisabeth Irwin High School in 1956. Two teachers encouraged her writing. The first was Hortense Eugenie Tyroler, an elegant and mysterious woman who taught her in seventh and eighth grades. Not only was Tyroler reputed to have a romantic past, but she was also known to be a professional ghostwriter. Norma envisioned her writing about spooky moors and Poesque marshes, only to discover later that Tyroler had actually been working on a book about scalp disease, to be published under the byline of a physician. The other influential teacher was Ed Stillman, who assigned creative writing projects in high school English. Under his tutelage, Klein stopped writing juvenile narratives about talking animals and discovered what, even today, she recognizes as her forte: "low-key descriptions of fairly everyday events: a fight with my brother, a school dance, a conflict with a friend."

Norma attended Cornell, Emanuel Klein's alma mater, for one year, before transferring to Barnard College, in large part to be back in New York City where she had a boyfriend. In 1960 she graduated Phi Beta Kappa and cum laude, no surprise to those who knew what a high achiever she had always been.

Partly in revolt against what she regarded as the unimaginative custom of majoring in English, so common to bright, middle-class young women, Klein decided to take her degree in Russian studies. She found the Russian novelists interesting and wanted to learn to read her favorite writer, Anton Chekhov, in the original. What better teacher for a future writer than the Russian master of literary objectivity, who, Klein discovered, could "get you so involved while he seems so detached." Later, after becoming a writer herself, she was to single out this Chekhovian quality as the peak of literary achievement. From the first, the Russian master intrigued her, showing her how the writing of narrative could be an art as powerfully refined and subtle as that of the dancer, painter, or musician.

Throughout college, she took creative writing classes, all of them from published writers: Robert Pack, W. D. Snodgrass, and George P. Elliott. Listening to her professors' shop talk, she learned the near impossibility of making a living from fiction writing alone. Since college teaching seemed the logical recourse, she entered a doctoral program in Slavic languages, with the intent of becoming a professor. But she soon found Slavic linguistics tiresome and draining of her creative energies. Since she had, in the meantime, fallen in love, she decided, most contrary to feminist doctrine, to let a man support her while she wrote fiction. Though she took an M.A. from Columbia University in 1963, she never finished her doctorate.

Klein first met Erwin Fleissner when she was twenty-one and entering her senior year at Barnard. He had graduated from Yale three years earlier and was just returning from England, where he had spent two years as a Rhodes scholar. When they met, he was beginning his doctoral studies in biochemistry at Columbia.

Fleissner was the American-born son of German immigrant parents. His mother came from a Lutheran family tradition, while his father's family background was Roman Catholic. The elder Fleissners, Else and Otto, had spent their adult lives teaching German at Wells, a small women's college in Aurora, New York, a hamlet with about three hundred inhabitants. Erwin had first attended the local one-room schoolhouse, before moving on to Deerfield and Yale. By the time Klein met him, he had prep school and Ivy League polish, and she was, by her own admission, attracted by the very "waspishness" of his physique, dress, and temperament. She also intuitively sensed that his more collected demeanor would nicely complement her own temperament. She describes him, even today, as "thoughtful, reflective, held back" while she is, by her own accounting, "intense and volatile." Yet they quickly discovered shared values on important matters: religion (they were agnostic), politics (liberal), art (they liked it), and family (which they soon decided they wanted). After living together for over three years, they were legally married in 1963 by a Unitarian minister in New Haven. Neither the Kleins nor the Fleissners had German or Jewish antipathies; different though their backgrounds were, they expressed their approval of the marriage.

Klein, who had already determined to be a writer, believed that successful women writers had rarely been mothers. She had carefully read her Virginia Woolf, and she was alert to the importance of having a room of her own and few distractions. Since Erwin was also, in those first years, totally absorbed in his work, they waited four years before having the first of their two daughters. Considering the high divorce rate, especially among women in the arts and professions, some may regard Norma Klein's successful marriage of twenty-plus years as an even more enviable achievement than her celebrity as a novelist. Klein acknowledges that she has indeed been fortunate in the close relationships she has maintained with the men in her life: first her father and brother and later her husband.

Erwin Fleissner is a successful man in his own right, with a career in cancer research at the Sloan-Kettering Institute. Recently he has become Dean of Sciences and Mathematics at Hunter College. Though he is not an avid reader of fiction, he is constantly supportive of his wife's career. He is wise enough never to criticize her books to excess, yet, at the same time, he has been able to provide helpful suggestions and make perceptive observations. For example, after he read the first novel she wrote from the point of view of a young male, he was able to reassure her that she had been thoroughly convincing. Professional critics and, even more importantly, readers, soon concurred. She respects his judgment and knows that he tells her the truth, however tactfully.

Her favorable experience with men has given Klein a benevolence toward them that has caused some people, ironically, to question her commitment to feminism. She has never been anti-male, and she sees no necessary conflict between a happy marriage, the care of children, and a woman's self-realization. The male characters in her fiction, whatever their ages, are usually likable (she prefers the adjective *thoughtful* to describe them) individuals who respect women. She acknowledges that many of the more attractive fathers who have appeared in her novels have been based on a combination of her own father and husband. At the same time, she admits that her own experience with men has been limited and is perhaps atypical. As a self-employed person, she has not been forced to compete with them in the office or to deal with them as a subordinate. The men she knows socially are those she has chosen for their congenial qualities.

Both her husband and children have sometimes found Klein strident in the expression of her opinions. "There she goes again" is a comment she has heard many times from them, as she has mounted a new soapbox. Yet they are tolerant, if somewhat more restrained in their personal styles. Erwin Fleissner is, for example, a scientist, more concerned with nuclear disarmament than with the social and personal issues that his wife examines in her fiction.

Like their father and grandfather, the daughters have been important influences on both Klein's life and her writing. Their adventures and the experiences and personalities of their friends have sometimes provided models for her plots and characters. When they were children, she was more inclined to write juvenile stories than she is now. As they grew up, she found herself writing more about older teenagers. Now that Jennifer is at Yale, Klein's protagonists, she discovers, are likely to be graduating from high school or planning for higher education. Her daughters have also been helpful to Klein in even more immediate and practical ways:

Sadie and Emanuel Klein in the 1930s.

Norma held by her father, Emanuel, in 1939.

Emanuel Klein

Norma at ten in 1948.

Norma in high school, 1954.

Norma on her honeymoon, 1963.

Else and Otto Fleissner.

Norma in graduate school, 1964.

Victor Klein and daughter Emily, 1986.

Jen and Katie, 1987.

Erwin and Norma, 1987.

from time to time she has hired them to type her manuscripts. They have sometimes served as first readers of her fiction, and their suggestions have been gratefully accepted. When they were young, they were impressed by their mother's celebrity. Now that they are older, predictably, they seem less awed by her achievement.

When Jennifer as an infant served as model for the genial baby in *Give Me One Good Reason*, the critics complained that Klein had been too easy on her unmarried mother protagonist by providing such a trouble-free baby. Klein now cautions any reader likely to make inferences that her daughters do not much resemble the usual heroines of her young adult novels. For one thing, they are not, she insists, as sexually adventuresome as most of her fictional characters. After reading her books, Jennifer and Katherine frequently tease their mother by asking, "When is all this going to happen to us?"

Klein feels that the family environment she has provided has given her daughters healthy attitudes toward sexuality; they are restrained in their own conduct, prudent in their choices. She admits that one reason she has enjoyed writing about the sexual adventures of young people is that she herself was so inhibited in youth. In *Domestic Arrangements* and *Breaking Up* she has written about teenagers most unlike the Norma Klein who came of age in the fifties, who was timid and fearful. Yet in *Taking Sides* and "My Life as a Body" (soon to be published) she has indeed written about young people much like herself.

Jennifer Fleissner, the elder daughter, was born in 1967. She was, according to her mother, "fat, jolly, verbal, calm, fascinated by the world, responsive"—in short, the ideal infant for a busy mother who had career plans. Katherine, born three and a half years later, quickly revealed herself to be "a blithe spirit, intense, artistic." Now that both have reached young adulthood, they have demonstrated clear talents and penchants. "Jen," as she is known by her family, has written poetry, some of which has been published. In *The Queen of the What Ifs* her mother acknowledges the use of her poems. But Jen also shares the scientific interests of her father and now has a double major in literature and science at Yale. She is presently considering a career as an English professor but hopes to write on the side.

Katherine, or "Katie," currently wants to be an artist, poet, or psychologist. Though she attends a high school that specializes in music and art, she also writes very well. Klein believes that either of her daughters could succeed as a writer, each with her own distinctive style and preoccupations. She sees her daughters as a study in contrast; Jen is intellectual, while Katie is more emotional and intense.

In addition to her supportive family, Klein has been fortunate in her friends. She is herself a good friend, reliable, generous with her time, understanding, and intellectually stimulating. A number of her friends, including Judy Blume, Betty Miles, and Merrill Joan Gerber, are writers. Often Klein submits her writing to them and receives professional pointers, which she frequently heeds.

Though she admits it is difficult to be objective about people who are her personal friends as well as writing colleagues, Norma Klein has a number of favorite authors in the young adult and adult fields. She is generous in her evaluations of many of those who might be considered rivals. Her favorite authors of young adult fiction are Richard Peck, Betty Miles, Norma Fox Mazer, Harry Mazer, Judy Blume, Robert Cormier, Zibby O'Neal, and Deborah Hautzig. Klein admires Fox Mazer's realistic fiction, which she also finds "very poetic and special." She believes that Fox Mazer is one of the relatively few young adult writers who has produced "wonderful" short stories, some of them based on her Jewish family heritage. Klein also admires the genuine "wholesomeness" and absence of cant in the books of Miles. Cormier is a literary artist of serious stature whose work Klein likes because it embodies interesting ideas. Cormier is important to her because he is "hard hitting" and has opened doors in the young adult field. By contrast, Klein also admires the whimsical and highly imaginative drawings of Rosemary Wells.

Although she acknowledges a certain "sibling rivalry" with Blume, Klein remains a leading promoter of Blume's work. She respects the frankness characteristic of Blume's writing, though she does not believe that Blume has consciously intended to break taboos. *Forever* is one of Klein's favorites, not only of Blume's books but of all young adult fiction. Klein feels that both she and Blume have been hurt by the criticism that their work is "tasteless." Though they are always being compared, Klein affirms that the differences in their work are as striking as their similarities. Whereas Blume writes most often about middle-class junior high girls living in the suburbs, Klein has developed as her specialty stories about older, more intellectual urban teenagers. Increasingly, her novels are written from a male viewpoint, which Blume attempted only once, in *Then Again, Maybe I Won't*.

Though generous in her estimation of writers she admires, Klein is far from uncritical when she views young adult literature as a whole. Most of it is of lower literary quality than the best adult contemporary fiction, she believes. It is sometimes difficult for her to find one book that she would wholeheartedly recommend to her friends. She believes that people who work in the juvenile and young adult fields are frequently more constrained when it comes to writing about complex topics than their adult fiction counterparts. Klein believes that writing for young people has appealed to many librarians and teachers who are afraid of the darker side of life and of expressions of sexuality. The field has been seen as "a safe haven in which personal neurotic tendencies were glorified, in fact were a plus."

When Klein attends American Library Association conventions she meets many people working professionally in young adult literature who appear to her to read little outside their own field. While they may know juvenile and young adult books, they rarely seem well read in mainstream fiction or literary history. "They seem to want to hide in a bland, one-dimensional, sexless world," she observes. There is also a gushing, uncritical approach toward what is liked; too much "sweetness and light" is admired, and the toughness of genuine literature is not always praised when it appears.

Klein's very entry into the field was in partial response to her perception of its low quality and its neglect of significant issues. Concerned with the books given her own children, she felt young people deserved better and more realistic books than they were getting. Despite the success she has had with her own subsequent books, she still sometimes finds juvenile and young adult literature too isolated a vineyard in which to labor. It is still dominated by women, with a resulting lack of prestige. Other writing colleagues, with whom Klein frequently converses as a member of the Author's Guild and PEN, still tend to think of juvenile fiction authors as folk who write about "little bunnies," who have not found the courage to dare writing for adults.

While she was growing up, Klein often thought of becoming a visual artist. Since her own nursery school days, she has frequently spent mornings of leisure drawing and painting. By the time Jen was in kindergarten, Klein was reading dozens of picture books to her. Friends were always suggesting that she should illustrate children's books, and she finally decided to try. After putting together several picture book texts accompanied by her own illustrations, she approached a book agent. His response was not encouraging. While she was an amateur of some talent, he told her frankly, her art work was not professional enough to be seriously considered by publishers. Anyhow, publishers were looking for realistic contemporary novels about children eight to twelve years of age, rather than picture books.

Klein made a trip to the public library and surveyed the field. The general quality of realistic fiction for eight- to twelve-year-olds did not seem high. Since she had already written short stories for adults, she felt eager to attempt a book in this genre. After she had proven herself by publication, she hoped that publishers would then let her illustrate her own picture books. With these motivations, and after quickly determining what the conventions of the genre were, she wrote *Mom, the Wolf Man and Me* in two weeks. It was her initial experience with first-person narrative, which she selected because the genre seemed to require it. She found the relaxed, colloquial style creatively liberating, and she also discovered that she liked the shorter length of juvenile fiction. Writing a book for young people was not so very unlike writing a short story. Upon its publication, the almost immediate success of *Mom, the Wolf Man and Me,* as well as the uproar it created, made it clear to her that she had found a niche. Though she was never allowed to illustrate a picture book (and she was soon so busy writing narrative that she lost interest anyhow), she was well on her way to becoming a leading author of juvenile and young adult fiction.

Klein is now firmly established as a writer, with all her energies channeled into her narratives. She no longer thinks about entering the art field, though she still enjoys making collages with shapes cut from magazines, connected with her black india ink drawings. These collages, made into calendars, are presented to friends at holiday time. Quiet Sunday mornings are now set aside for art projects, a relaxing activity at the family weekend retreat outside the city.

Klein feels that despite the good work of the colleagues she names, the majority of juvenile books still do not achieve high literary standards. In fact, the very books that appeal to teachers and win awards from associations of librarians, she believes, are likely to be those that "children wouldn't read if you tied them to the bedpost." The situations dealt with in these books, which are considered to have such high literary merit, are generally set in the 1860s and can be summed up in a series of questions: "Shall I go to the well? Will the Indians attack?" Klein denounces "these dead, dead books," which so often impress adults. They are favorably judged by the reviewers of the specialized journals, who often seem themselves, according to Klein, to have been "born in 1819 mentally." Historical romance, a category into which many of these books fall, more often than not transmits a false view of the past and reinforces sexist stereotypes, she maintains.

Not only has Klein read widely and critically in the young adult field, but she is also equally knowledgeable about contemporary adult fiction, where she also, from time to time, continues to make a contribution. Writers she admires in the adult field include Margaret Drabble, Hilma Wolitzer, Alice Adams, Cynthia Propper Seaton, and Anne Tyler. From her lists of favorite writers, it seems clear that Klein enjoys the work of polished stylists who do not write in the heroic mode but choose to present the nuances of everyday life, with humor and sometimes with a slight touch of whimsy. Her favorite writers are those who have "the feminine sensibility," who savor the details of the experiences that are most common to women.

Sometimes, Klein believes, it is not beneficial for a writer to become the object of intense, even though favorable, critical attention. Her conversation reveals an almost superstitious fear of sustained critical adulation, even while she laments that serious critics have usually neglected the juvenile and young adult fields. She has now almost given up the hope she once held that professional critics would be constructive guides, much like "very good English teachers." She also regards with some trepidation the dangers that great success can present to a writer's private life. People may start taking themselves too seriously, she believes, when Hollywood buys movie rights for hundreds of thousands of dollars or when they are discovered by some elite literary coterie.

Though Klein speaks most frequently of contemporary writers when she is discussing what she likes and dislikes in literature, she still acknowledges the influence of earlier authors she studied in college. As a former student of Russian literature, she is aware of the importance of those giants of the novel, Dostoevsky and Tolstoy, yet she does not discover in them kindred spirits. She was influenced by the simplicity of Hemingway's style, particularly in his early short stories, and is admiring of D. H. Lawrence for his openness in writing about sexuality and his lyric, intense vision.

In addition to Chekhov, who remains her favorite writer, Klein has learned much from Jane Austen. The lives of extraordinary women have always interested Klein, and no one seems more unusual to her than Austen, who, lacking much formal education, might be said to have created the modern novel. Though Austen traveled little and had few adventures, she made superb fiction from the material provided by her limited environment. Another woman intriguing to Klein, who, by contrast, had a life filled with exotic experiences, is Margaret Mead. While Mead did not write fiction, her prolific and dramatic presentations of anthropological theories and findings brought that discipline to a mass public. Though some of Mead's work has recently been challenged, Klein still admires her, because Mead broke the old rules and had the audacity to promulgate new ones.

Klein is a quick study and a fast writer. Sometimes her novels are produced so rapidly that errors and inconsistencies of detail are not corrected in the finished drafts. Pointing out these minor inconsistencies has become a favorite activity of reviewers. Although she rarely writes more than six months of the year, Klein's mind is always working. She finds ideas for her plots everywhere. She has even learned to use the creative power of the subconscious mind. Sometimes she dreams up her plots while waiting for the bus or starts out the day with the germ of an idea and discovers it to be well formulated by evening. She enjoys lunching regularly with friends in Manhattan restaurants. From their conversations she also picks up good story ideas. Like many lifetime New Yorkers, Klein does not drive and fears that if she did she might drive off a cliff while mentally developing a plot. She has also been known to take the basic ideas for her books from films, plays, and novels.

Klein finds writing an intense experience, and she sometimes gets emotionally involved in the exploits of her characters. When her protagonists start developing their own volitions, as their chronicler she hastily follows them and sometimes has to bail them out of difficulties. She genuinely likes almost all the personalities who people her pages and is capable of giving a mother's impassioned defense of them.

Since she is her own boss, Klein understands that discipline and self-motivation are essential. Early on, even with her first book, she established her method of writing, which has changed very little. She composes on an electric typewriter, and has so far resisted the promptings of other writers to get a word processor. She neither likes nor understands machines, and word processors seem as alien to her as automobiles. She types at least five pages a day and sometimes as many as fifteen. Five is usually too few, while ten pages is a good morning's work of two or three hours. She likes to leave afternoons free for walking, lunching with friends, or seeing old movies, an activity she especially loves. At the end of each day, she rereads the pages of the morning and pencils in small changes. Her early drafts are very good, and few corrections are usually needed. She is no Flaubert-style writer, who struggles to find *le mot juste,* but a narrator who easily achieves a clear, utilitarian style. Later, after her editor has made suggestions, she may make further alterations in her manuscript before publication. Usually these are minor and few.

When she begins a book, Klein has already worked out the central conflict and is likely to have constructed mentally the first and last scenes, as well as plotted out several others. Since her books are written for a particular audience and often for a familiar publisher, she usually knows in advance the approximate length that is expected. When the main character is eleven or twelve, publishers expect one hundred to one hundred twenty-five pages; for a teenage novel they will rarely accept more than two hundred pages, while three to five hundred is considered appropriate for an adult novel. Though she usually conforms to these expectations, Klein realizes they are riddled with contradictions. The same teenager who is not expected to purchase a young adult book of over two hundred pages will devour a protracted novel like *Gone with the Wind* from a parent's library. Yet market analysis dominates publishing. Klein's books have occasionally been placed on the adult lists merely because of their length or sexual explicitness, or both.

Klein's income, in addition to that of her husband, is essential to the family's urban life-style. While maintaining the writing schedule necessary to make a good living, Klein can be versatile as well as prolific. Though she makes adjustments from time to time, a frequent pattern is to write a teenage novel in October, a month in the city she particularly savors. She is happy in the fall, enjoying the change from hot summer. Then she usually takes a vacation until January. During the winter months she may write an adult novel, say from January to March. After that, there is another vacation until late June. In summertime the heat saps her enthusiasm and Klein, despite her unusually high energy level, says, "I only feel up to a short novel in the summer, so it's then that I write a book for younger children." She has obviously mastered the technique of time management.

Since her husband is tied to an eleven-month-a-year job, she does not venture forth between books for exotic vacations. Although as a teenager she made bicycle trips in France and England and visited Russia during a youth festival in 1957, she is not much of a traveler these days. When she goes to England now, it is for a few days to promote her books, which are beginning to catch on there. Instead of traveling during her free periods, she does paperwork, answers fan mail, and makes herself available for speaking engagements. Writing, which requires intense concentration, is demanding work, both physically and emotionally, and she feels the need for these breaks. Even so, Klein has an enormous output. During the breaks, she also starts gathering the ideas for the next season's crop of novels.

Though her career got off to a splendid start with *Mom, the Wolf Man and Me* and has maintained its momentum since, Klein has nevertheless experienced some disappointments and frustrations. She has now largely given up short story writing, which she liked very much, because she found it financially unprofitable and because she decided that novels allow her greater room to explore her characters' feelings. Unless a writer is able to sell regularly to the *New Yorker,* there is little recognition, she feels, for the short story. Stories are published in little magazines that pay meagerly and can rarely accommodate any substantial length. There is no large readership, and the attention the stories receive is ephemeral. The best one can expect is to make an O. Henry Award collection, which Klein's stories have done, or to be published by a small, prestigious university press. Except for *New Yorker* collections, anthologies are never profitable for the writer who earns her living by her pen.

Another frustration for Klein has been the art work that accompanies her picture books. She has rarely been pleased with these illustrations and has had little control over the choice of artists and styles of work. When *Girls Can Be Anything* was published she found that the illustrations, which she calls "cartoony and sexist," even contradicted the central message of the text. Perhaps only in *Visiting Pamela* did Klein find the skilled and appealing pictures by Kay Chorao truly satisfying. By the time this book was published (1979), Klein had acquired enough clout with her publishers to demand a major illustrator. Echoing in these complaints is some of the disappointment of the frustrated artist. When Klein speaks of her friend Rosemary Wells, who alternates between drawing picture books and writing fiction, there is a touch of gentle envy as well as admiration.

The covers of the paperback editions of her novels have also displeased Klein. With their garish and sentimental scenes, they sometimes seem designed to entrap the casual reader rather than to capture the attention of the serious one. The covers frequently make the books difficult to distinguish on bookstore shelves from formula romances and series books of dubious quality.

Klein takes her readers seriously and enjoys receiving letters from them. She seems especially pleased when young people quite unlike the characters in her books—readers who do not come from the urban upper middle class or the eastern intellectual centers of the country—tell her they find her books meaningful. While the bulk of her readers are still from the East or from Texas—probably because Texans have had more money to indulge themselves in books, she reasons—more and more readers are turning up in places like Arkansas and Alabama. They find her stories of family life in New York City exotic and enjoy her books much in the way she, as a child growing up in the city, was intrigued by the midwestern, turn-of-the-century family stories of Maude Hart Lovelace, whose Betsy, Tacy, and Tib books were among her juvenile favorites. While most of Klein's fan mail comes from ten- to fourteen-year-old girls, she is pleased when older or younger people tell her they like her books. A fan letter from a young male reader is perhaps the most prized of all, being relatively rare.

She strongly objects to the rigid packaging and marketing that takes place in publishing. A good book, regardless of the age of its protagonists, should have some appeal to all people with literary sensitivity, regardless of age or sex. Books for the young do not have to be morally didactic, educational, or therapeutic. Only a dull book is a bad one, she insists, whether written for children, young adults, or adults. Klein believes in reading across categories. The "crossover," just as desired in publishing as it is in the recording industry, is all too rare. She believes that those who write and publish mainstream adult fiction are wrong in scorning juvenile and young adult literature, just as professionals in the field of juvenile literature make a mistake by reading too few adult novels. Klein, who states her opinions forcefully, has said: "I wish more adults outside the children's book field were willing to read young adult books. We live in an age where everything must be packaged and marketed. It infuriates me that my work is always seen as potentially for teenagers, even if my main character is an eighty-year-old man."

She believes that more serious novels need to be written about teenage boys, from their point of view. The sports story and the "hot rod genre," generally thought to appeal to the young male audience, have long ago been played out. The personal relationships of young men need to be explored more in fiction, as they were so effectively, Klein believes, in *The Catcher in the Rye*. How do teenage males feel about sex, their families, school, the future, even pregnant girlfriends? Unwed pregnancy has generally been regarded in fiction, as in life, as a young woman's problem. But a few unwed fathers have asserted in the courts that they too have rights. These men obviously have feelings about their children, born or unborn, even when deprived of legal rights. Such feelings need to be sensitively explored in fiction. As Klein has found herself writing more and more about such problems from the young male's point of view, she has discovered a special, highly satisfying objectivity that she was unable to attain before, when using young females as her first-person narrators.

C. S. Lewis claimed that he chose the children's tale because it was the appropriate genre for the sort of story he wished to tell. Similarly Klein appears to have chosen the young adult narrative most frequently because she finds its length congenial and its appropriate topics and themes those that most interest her. One such theme is the passage of time and its effect on human lives. Adolescence is a period of transition, and the transitions of life hold particular fascination as potential crisis points. "Teenagers, I think," Klein has said, "live more in the present; their life's history is short, and the future seems endless." The future also seems ripe with possibilities. At no other period in life, Klein believes, does an individual experience life so keenly or perceive it so much as an exploration.

Klein does not want to write the kind of escapist fiction that is cranked out chiefly for cash. Though the money she makes from writing remains important to her family and herself, Klein is never ready to put aside artistic considerations. She has no interest in the suspense narrative or the fantasy, two favorite escapist genres. Her commitment, she has emphatically stated, is to real life.

Though Klein obviously loves her trade and feels that she has been fortunate in being able to earn a living as her own boss, doing what she most enjoys, she is well aware of the hazards of writing. A good writer may dry up, may write herself out. When this happens, it is difficult for even the most successful and acclaimed writers—perhaps especially so for them—to find other work. When prospective employers see "twenty novels published" on a resumé, they are not impressed; on the contrary, they may even be suspicious that the candidate will be a dreamy artist, unfit for ordinary work. Klein's personal experience has already revealed this to her. When she once applied for a job away from her writing desk, she found that potential employers were totally unimpressed by the statistics of her book sales.

Yet the rewards of writing are also unique. "As a writer you lead a thousand lives," Klein has said. "In real life most writers are shy, introverted people who have anxiety attacks crossing the street against the light. But in our books we murder people off, we defeat our enemies, we change the world. For a male or female Walter Mitty, that's terrific."

Norma Klein is conscientious about answering her fan mail and makes herself available to talk to those who work seriously in the field of juvenile fiction. People who know her only from a superficial reading of her books or through her reputation as "controversial" report that they are sometimes surprised when they meet her, expecting an assertive Gloria Steinem sort of individual. She exudes warmth and joy when approaching her public and friends. People who meet her even for the first time are impressed by her friendliness and good humor, by her animation, quick wit, and responsiveness. Unlike some celebrities whose stock in trade is being articulate, she does not "hold forth," but really converses with people.

Yet Klein does not deny that she is opinionated. While she can be reasonable and thoughtful in the expression of ideas important to her, she can also be intemperate. She admits that she sometimes makes emphatic statements that are based on quick impressions rather than on careful reasoning.

Regarding feminism as the basic issue of the time, she feels women have always faced harsh discrimination, and the exercise of their talents has been severely curtailed in almost all human societies. She worries that her own daughters will suffer from coming of age in what she regards as a still sexist society. She is particularly troubled by recent studies documenting the difficulty that intelligent, educated women have in finding suitable husbands. Men are put off "even by women who get C's at the University of Miami," she observes, in a typical Kleinism. The fact that American men tend, according to studies, to want to marry down rather than find women who are intellectual equals is a matter of real concern to Klein, who values her own relationships with men and hopes her daughters will be equally fortunate.

Though she takes considerable pride in her Jewish heritage, Klein likes to tell people, "it was almost inevitable that I marry a Gentile." The man who became her husband first impressed her as a WASP intellectual, a type she found appealing and slightly exotic. She has little use for organized religion of any kind, indicting Judaism along with all other great world religions for sexism and bigotry. Such a sweeping condemnation, needless to say, is another example of her tendency to oversimplify complex issues. Nevertheless, despite her problems with the Jewish religion, she feels that positive attitudes have resulted from her own heritage. It is no accident, she believes, that she and Judy Blume, both from Jewish backgrounds, are the writers most known for iconoclasm in young adult literature. Being Jewish in the Western world tends to give one a certain objectivity, that perspective of the outsider looking into the convoluted lives of the rest of society, which can be so useful to a writer. On questionnaires Klein continues to give her religion as "none." Yet she acknowledges a sense of disappointment when she recently asked her daughters if they regarded themselves as Jewish and they replied, "Not particularly." This ambivalence, a certain wistfulness for a rejected spiritual heritage, surfaces most intriguingly in her writing.

The sexual revolution attracted national attention in the sixties. Though many of its effects may turn out to be temporary and exaggerated by the media, it has certainly led to a loosening of sexual restraints throughout the Western world, even to a degree in American small towns and rural areas. The wide, if not quite universal, acceptance of "living together," along with the gay rights movement, have been important and controversial topics in Klein's writing. She welcomes the disappearance of the sexual restraints of previous eras and the increased tolerance of individual freedom and choice. Yet she acknowledges herself to be fairly conventional in her own life-style, as a married woman and mother.

Klein feels it is her right and perhaps her obligation to deal with the importance of sexuality in the lives of adolescents. Her books present problems to those librarians and teachers who must confront a public often oblivious to the values of literature and confused about their own sexual standards. It is chiefly because of their sexual openness, as well as their frank language, that several of Klein's books have become the targets of censorship. Though many of the books have called forth some protests—*Mom, the Wolf Man and Me* usually comes first to mind—the two that have been most attacked are *Naomi in the Middle*, written for younger children, and *It's OK If You Don't Love Me*, now more safely published on the adult lists, though rather obviously written for and about teenagers. There has even been some objection to *Sunshine*, a fictionalization for adults of material that had already appeared successfully on television. Klein has observed with considerable irony that the same people who protest a book that will be read by only a relatively limited audience of young people will tolerate identical material on a television program viewed by millions.

Klein's books have never been salacious; they lack the leering and titillating quality essential to pornography. Klein will also never be among the great erotic writers; a sense of the grand cosmic dimension of sexuality is absent from her work. Even her friends have told her, "Your books may be about sex, but they are not sexy books." In her fiction Klein has never appeared very interested in the physiology of sex; she is concerned with sexuality as a fact of life, one of the major problems and central discoveries of the teen years, when most young people are obsessed with the mystery of sexuality in all its problematic complexity. Books about teenagers are absurd if they are not permitted to acknowledge this fact. As a daughter of a Freudian analyst, it is not surprising that Klein would be especially conscious of the importance of sexuality. However, sexual experience for her characters, even if it is not part of a deeper commitment, is never merely a physical act. It is part of each individual's quest for meaning. In Klein's books it is the interactions between personalities and not the sexual encounters themselves that are most interesting.

Klein has dealt charitably with both gay men and lesbians in her writing, and in real life she respectfully accepts them among her friends and colleagues. In the last fifteen years, she is only one of several writers to introduce homosexuality, matter-of-factly and nonjudgmentally, into books for young people. The lesbian mother in *Breaking Up* is presented sympathetically, as is the gay friend of the heroine in "My Life as a Body" (not yet published). Klein also hopes to write a novel from the point of view of a gay teenager.

Klein has said that she believes in struggling for justice and liberation, even though she ultimately has little hope for the human race. "I have a funny view," she has said, "because I believe one has to devote one's life to changing the world, and yet I think it will never change. It is an existential thing. . . . I don't believe people should retreat and say it doesn't matter who they vote for; I believe we should fight every inch of the way. But I also believe that the world is going to go up in smoke." This despair, however, is rarely if ever evident in her work, which is basically optimistic, even humanistic, in its affirmation. In Klein's books the reader encounters little of the painful groping of humanity without God in a universe that does not honor reason, the philosophical stance of a Sartre or a Camus, to name the most famous existential novelists. It is difficult to escape the impression that Klein articulates a philosophical position that she cannot temperamentally accept.

Klein has been praised for her pioneering literary spirit, her courage in venturing forth where others have not very boldly stepped, yet she has also been chastized for certain limitations to her sympathy and subject matter. In more recent books she has left behind her characteristic subject, the upper middle-class urban young woman. More and more, young males have become her central characters and first-person narrators. Blacks and people who live in places other than New York City have also appeared. Klein has occasionally ventured fictionally into Canada and Europe, though without great verisimilitude of detail. She is a prolific writer in midcareer. Her writings clearly reflect her background as a well-educated New York woman of the Jewish upper middle class. The daughter of professional people, of liberal thinkers, she recognizes herself as an intellectual too, though she is at the same time an impulsive and feeling person, frequently more passionate than reflective in her judgments. While her first fiction may have been about people much like herself, her writing has attempted, with growing success, to reflect a broader social panorama. Though she continues to be known chiefly for her young adult fiction, it should never be forgotten that Klein has also distinguished herself by her books for young children and adults. It is now possible for a reader to move through the various stages of life with an appropriate Klein novel for entertainment and, sometimes, instruction. More and more, readers are certain to discover how reassuring it can be to grow up with a favorite writer, who seems like a friend from childhood and yet does not vanish when childhood is past.

2. Children's Books: "Non-punitive, Open, Honest"

The delightful picture books Norma Klein wrote while her own children were young were well received. Though she quickly realized that the picture book is an artist's medium, where an author is reduced to the writing of captions, Klein demonstrated a talent that included a substantial measure of the whimsy essential for success in this limited but specialized field. The books have had ample circulation, have been reprinted in inexpensive paperback editions, and are still on library shelves. They continue to be enjoyed by children themselves and remain pleasant for adults to read to children.

Klein has clearly stated her goal in producing children's books: "We need books where children masturbate, think about their parents' sex lives, enjoy the physical sensations provided by their bodies. We need books that are non-punitive, open, honest."[1] Though the picture book for young children obviously provides fewer opportunities for a writer to explore or promote ideas she considers important, Klein's work did bear her characteristic stamp and managed to express her "message." It was important to her that children be reached at the earliest age with the ideas she regards as healthy. Her interest in psychology, particularly the Freudian view of the sexuality of children, is as evident in these books as it has been in her writings for older audiences. Though the sexual curiosity of children is not often explored in books for the very young, Klein feels its treatment is beneficial to the development of the young reader. Because children in Klein books realistically speculate about their parents' sexuality and share misinformation, some adults have, predictably, decided these writings are unsuitable for public library shelves. It is not surprising that these narratives for and about younger children have been among the most controversial of all Klein's books.

Girls Can be Anything, the first picture book, was published in 1973. The illustrations by Roy Doty did not please Klein, who felt them inappropriate to the text. The cartoon-style drawings not only lacked the poetry of fine juvenile illustrations, but, in depicting mothers and fathers in traditional roles, they contradicted the nonsexist message of the text. Klein's point was precisely that little girls need not limit their ambitions. They may grow up to be queens, or prime ministers such as Indira Gandhi or Golda Meir; they may also choose from a variety of careers, including human or veterinary medicine. While the illustrations were not to the author's liking, some of the book's readers, both young and old, have been entertained by them, finding that they add a pleasing element of comedy to what might otherwise have come across as an overly didactic sermon.

The text is a dialogue between two kindergarten friends, Adam and Marina. Young Adam has already absorbed clear sex role stereotypes, and Marina has to explain to him that girls need not always be the nurses, in play or in real life, serving boys who are the doctors. Girls and boys alike may grow up to have such interesting jobs as driving buses and piloting planes. With Marina's patient instruction, Adam learns that a boy may even aspire to be the husband of a president of the United States. Klein considered *Girls Can Be Anything* to be such an important statement that she dedicated it to "Jenny" Fleissner, her elder daughter, who, in childhood, outlined her plans to grow up to be "a painter, a circus performer, and a soda jerk in a Baskin-Robbins ice-cream parlor."

Klein's second picture book was *Dinosaur's Housewarming Party,* published the next year. It is a slim tale within the animal fable tradition, perhaps an example of the stories Klein wrote as a child, before she came to appreciate realistic writing under the influence of her high school English teachers. The illustrations by James Marshall are pleasantly amusing, though their vivid colors and simple lines are designed to appeal more to very young children than to adults. An octopus types with four typewriters simultaneously and, later, is shown in bed easily eating toast, drinking tea, and reading a paper all at once with his many limbs. Though the book is not obviously preachy, it certainly conveys the lesson that one must accept the individuality and attributes, however eccentric, of others. The beast fable tradition, of which most children's animal fantasies are a part, always depicts "ourselves in fur," and Klein's animals do pointedly exhibit human failings as well as human compassion.

Dinosaur has been forced to move from his Greenwich Village apartment because his neighbors were always complaining that his tail obstructed their view and he was constantly knocking down their clotheslines with his bulk and clumsiness. His friends, including Green Worm, Octopus, and Wanda the Warthog, show up to "warm" his new apartment. They bring appropriate gifts, such as a plant and an inflatable vinyl chair. Through their acceptance of his ungainly presence and their understanding of dinosaur needs, they help him overcome his feelings of rejection.

Though the story is slim, it appealed to young children because of the attractively odd collection of anthropomorphic animals and because of the clever pictures by an artist who understood precisely what children find funny. Klein also demonstrated her ability to turn out another charming trifle. Any author, no matter how successful otherwise, who has ever tried such writing knows how difficult it is.

If I Had My Way, also published in 1974, was a more ambitious fantasy exploration of childhood wishes. Little Ellie sees that adults dominate children by their capricious instructions and decides a reversal is in order. In dreamland, where all things are possible, everything is turned topsy-turvy; children are suddenly in control, with adults subject to their whims. The clever text and matching illustrations provide both wish fulfillment for children and amusement for adults who may be reading the book to them. Though it contained no expletives or speculations on the sexual practices of grownups, features that usually cause difficulty for Klein's books, there were still adults who failed to respond to the whimsy of the book and declared its premise objectionable. Consequently, it was removed from some public library shelves. Klein quickly learned a lesson librarians and teachers know well; the uses of fantasy are beyond the comprehension of some prosaic minds. Educators learn very early that unsophisticated parents may object as strongly to juvenile adaptations of Homer as to *The Catcher in the Rye.*

The book's illustrations work. Oranges and yellows dominate Ray Cruz's visualization of childhood frustration and wish fulfillment. Parents look quite funny showing their feelings of helplessness, when roles are suddenly reversed and children start telling them what to do, all the time scolding them for their inability to understand the sense of a constant barrage of instructions. What most critics did not observe in their reviews is that the book may have a stronger lesson for the adults reading it to children than for the children themselves.

In Ellie's dream, a baby is delivered to her door. Finding the baby unacceptable, she sends it back; six babies are in turn rejected in the same manner. Ellie has obviously concluded that adults are all too ready to accept troublesome infants when they appear, as it were, on the doorstep. The delivery man brings them in transparent boxes tied with ribbons. While she is cooking, Ellie demands to know if her mother has brushed her teeth. She prepares spinach and casserole for Mom's meal, while her own supper is hot dogs and brownies with chocolate sauce and ice cream. Daddy, who has been good, gets to lick the chocolate from the spoon. Outside, all the children are having a party. As a special treat for the adults, who are usually not allowed out after dark, one from each family may go to the playground. Mom and Dad have a fight over which one gets to go first. At bedtime Ellie tucks them both in and tells them to "settle down." They call her back because she has forgotten to say "sweet dreams." She then prepares her own bedtime snack, a chocolate ice cream sundae.

The next morning Ellie wakes up, her fantasy gone, as her mother calls her to get out of bed and dress for the day. Baby William, her little brother, is leaning over his crib conversing in babytalk, a sure sign she is back in the real world.

Naomi in the Middle, illustrated by Leigh Grant, was published the same year and dedicated to Judy Blume. The book is vintage Klein and continues to generate as much controversy as anything else she has written. Bobo, age nine, and Naomi, seven, are very close friends, as well as sisters. Bobo, as the firstborn, has certain prerogatives, such as the right to keep a pet rat. Though she does not possess the benefits of primogeniture, Naomi, who narrates the story, still enjoys her status as the family baby. Problems arise when the girls learn that mother is expecting a third child, and Naomi will soon lose her present advantage. Neither sister is pleased. Becoming more and more annoyed as they think about the changes soon to come in their family life, they speculate on where babies come from while they are taking their daily bath. They have learned from family conversation that a boy is expected, yet from their point of view a brother would present special problems. Naomi speculates on one of the difficulties:

> "Will he have a bath with us if he's a boy?" I asked Bobo when we were in the bath.
> "Maybe."
> "Then he might put his penis in our vagina," I said "That's what boys do."
> "They don't do that till they're much much older," Bobo said.

The third child turns out to be a girl, rather than the son Mom and Dad wanted so much. The family, of course, lovingly accepts her, and Bobo and Naomi quickly become reconciled to looking out for a still younger sister.

A Train for Jane, published by the Feminist Press the same year as *Naomi in the Middle,* is an excursion into verse, easy flowing and witty. The accompanying illustrations by Miriam Schottland, perhaps too expressionistic for most juvenile tastes, are old-fashioned inlays in valentine card style, with the colors of red and green set off against charcoal. The feminist message of the text is unmistakable, though presented with levity: there is no excuse for sexist toys. Jane wants a train for Christmas and will not settle for any of the attractive "girl" toys—the dollhouses, crystal beads, ballet slippers, lacy skirts, and so on—that her relatives suggest as appropriate. Jane cannot be dissuaded and in the end does find a train under the Christmas tree, a reward for her persistence.

Blue Trees, Red Sky (1975) was Klein's sixth picture book within a two-year period. The illustrations by Pat Grant Porter, if not exceptional, are attractive, in black and white except for the cover illustration, which is in charcoal, blue, and red. The book contains fifty-seven pages of pictures elucidating a slight plot. Relying chiefly for its appeal and humor on the conversations of two eight-year-olds, the text presents the interactions between Valerie, her friend Leah, and Valerie's four-year-old brother, Marco.

The message again is clear: gainful employment may be as important to a woman's self-identity and esteem as it is to a man's, and it is well for children to learn this early. Valerie, whose mother is a working widow, is always lonesome. She feels that Mrs. Weiss, the hired woman who takes care of the children, prefers brother Marco to her, and she longs for her mother to stay home and keep her company all day long. Mother's task is to explain that her work means far more to her than just the money it earns. Yet her love for her job does not detract from her dedication to her children nor her ability to provide proper care for them.

In any Klein book for young children, readers have come to expect some talk of sex or of "making pee pee." Valerie speaks once of washing her vagina. Strong stuff, many believe, for children's books! In Middle America, where thousands of parents will not even permit their children to be given a sexed doll, such books continue to cause consternation. The children in *Blue Trees, Red Sky* giggle as they make up rhymes such as: "I'm going to China to see your vagina" and "I'm going to Venus to see your penis." Mrs. Weiss observes, though without real disapproval, that she didn't even know such words at Valerie's age.

Mom has a boyfriend named George who likes the children and

may or may not at some future point become their stepfather. Though she vacations with George and keeps steady company with him, Mom is not sure whether or not she wants to marry him. Klein's adult world is never carefree, even as it is presented to juvenile audiences. At one point Valerie finds her mother lying on the couch looking sad; Mom admits she is thinking about Dad's death.

This book—which is certainly "open, honest, and non-punitive"—is an insight rather than a plot book. It introduces the reader to a happy single-parent family. The children, who are attractive yet not idealized, talk as children really do. Sentimentality, cuteness, and clichés are all avoided by both author and illustrator. Valerie comes to terms with her mother's reality as a person, a human being who exists outside the role of motherhood. Her needs for stimulating work outside the home and for adult male companionship, even sex, are as much a part of her nature as her desire to nurture her children and her grief over the loss of her husband.

Klein's last picture book, *Visiting Pamela,* was published by Dial in 1979 and illustrated by Kay Chorao, one of the most creative and gifted artists working in the juvenile field. By this time Klein was able to assert some of her own ideas about illustrations. The highly inventive interactions of illustrator and author make this perhaps the most attractive of Klein's picture books, even though the plot itself is thin. In family scenes, even the teddy bear and dolls scattered about the children's rooms have interesting, questioning expressions. For example, a dog eyes a visiting child with friendly curiosity, waiting to see if he will be accepted, while the hesitant child asks if he bites.

Carrie, age five, is a homebody. Her mother tells her to visit her friends' houses if she wishes them to continue coming to her own home. Reluctantly, Carrie, who does not like being separated from her toys and her cat, agrees to visit her chum Pamela. At Pamela's house she meets the family dog and baby Oscar, identified by his sister as a pest who chews things. Carrie, who knows that "sometimes without even telling you, mommies get fat and babies come out and you have to bring them home from the hospital," is nevertheless glad they do not have a baby at her house. She notes that the baby has an unpleasant smell.

Carrie is a finicky little girl who worries about the seeds in the grapes Pamela's babysitter gives them to eat. Thinking wistfully of the cookies she gets after school at her own house, she telephones her mother claiming that since Pamela's dog is trying to bite her she must come home immediately. By the time Mother arrives, however, Carrie is having a marvelous time playing with coloring books and eating the chocolate chip cookies Pamela has procured in the meantime. The two friends have dressed up in Batman clothes and are watching television while lying on Pamela's parents' bed. Carrie has decided that visiting can be fun after all.

This reassuring narrative captures the excitement of a mild adventure of childhood. Carrie is a bit of a prig, set in her ways, as indeed some little girls already are, particularly when they have the privileged position of "only child" in a family. Both Klein and Chorao appear to have been working from firsthand knowledge of children; the keen ear for their conversations and the keen eye for the nuances of their facial expressions make the book especially realistic. It requires considerable craft to convey personality so successfully and tell an amusing story purely through the actions and words of the characters, without obtrusive commentary. Yet it was the meeting of skilled narrator and first-class illustrator that really made this book a model for its genre.

A few of Norma Klein's books—with much longer narratives—have been classified as young adult fiction by her publishers though they are actually of more appeal to younger children. The classification of Klein's books remains a constant problem. A long-held belief in the juvenile field is that while younger children will read about older ones, they do not like reading about protagonists younger than themselves. Another prevalent belief is that girls will read books about the adventures of boys but boys do not enjoy books primarily about the problems and concerns of girls. Though there is certainly some truth in these contentions, the general success of several of Klein's books with both sexes and a wide range of ages has suggested that some reconsideration of the classification of youth books may be in order.

Confessions of an Only Child (1973) and its sequel, *Tomboy* (1978), are of primary interest to the subteen audience. Klein does not write series books, and it is unusual for her to carry characters over from one book to another. She claims she does not reread her books and frequently does not even remember her characters clearly enough to be interested in their subsequent adventures. Because *Tomboy* is in part a continuation of *Confessions,* it holds a unique place in the Klein canon and consequently both books deserve some scrutiny.

Confessions of an Only Child, which is competently illustrated by Richard Cuffari, provides a fuller and better story than *Naomi in the Middle.* It is also one of the most controversial of all the author's books. Klein's characteristic openness is evident throughout. There is speculation about the ways babies are born, by children who have already been told all—or almost all—by their parents. But the book's central event is the loss of Mother's baby, whom Toe Henderson, the young heroine, never wanted in the first place because she likes being an only child. Yet when the baby dies, Toe finds that she thoroughly shares the family grief. By the time another baby is born to take the place of the lost one, Toe has adjusted to the idea of sharing her parents' affections. The book shows considerable empathy with the plight of the child who must suddenly give place to a younger one, a plight with which many readers can identify. *Confessions* is another insight book of sincerity and some depth.

In *Tomboy* Toe already has a little brother, Brendan, along with two dogs she seems to value almost as much. One is elderly and belonged to Mother before her marriage. The dog has a painful accident and must be "put to sleep," to Mom's great distress. More serious family troubles ensue. Dad, an architect, loses his job. But he has flexibility and strong character and is able to adjust cheerfully to being a househusband for a while. He even develops special skill in taking care of Brendan. Dad comes to school when there is a program in which parents talk to the class about their professions. He explains what it is like taking care of a baby. Toe finds herself a little jealous, because, after all, Dad, whom she adores, had not been home to care for her when she was an infant. Mom, who is trained as a lawyer, has been fortunate enough in the meantime to find work to support the family. Toe remains happy; she is as secure as ever, despite the major role reversals of her parents.

Beginning to feel that she should also be doing her bit, Toe gets a job walking two neighborhood dogs. She finds that she enjoys the responsibility of caring for living creatures, and she learns other lessons as well. Though she dislikes rowdy behavior, she must accept her best friend Libby's tomboy phase. Another crisis comes when Toe gets her period early, at age eleven. She is not only frightened, but she is embarrassed for the androgynous Libby to know that she has matured so rapidly. Her mother is able to reassure her that she is merely following a familiar family pattern of early maturity.

Toe's family has still not forgotten the baby that died in the first book. The death of one of the dogs brings back some of the pain and emptiness they suffered at that time. But as a family group they have survived grief and have learned to deal with loss in a constructive fashion. It would be hard to find, anywhere in the juvenile or young adult sections of the public library, a more strongly pro-family book than *Tomboy*. Family support, the book says, not only enables young people to accept economic disruptions, grief, and loss, but also provides the reassurance needed to make the necessary transitions of life gracefully.

The two books about Toe Henderson are pleasantly lacking in pretentiousness. They read well, as do all Klein's narratives. If it is true, as some of the critics have asserted, that you get more problems than plot from these books,[2] at least the problems examined are meaningful ones: a young girl's concern with her developing body and her grief over the deaths of humans and animals.

Three other books, which take the problems of older children seriously, fall into the transitional category: *What It's All About*

(1975), *A Honey of a Chimp* (1980), and *Robbie and the Leap Year Blues* (1981).

What It's All About is one of Klein's strongest family stories. Bernadette Nakamura is an eleven-year-old whose father is Japanese-American, while her mother is Jewish-American. Her parents are now divorced and live at both ends of the continent, though they are still on good terms. Bernadette's babysitter is a young woman who is studying to be a rabbi. The child herself is a budding writer, working on her *Divorced Child's Cookbook* or her "Mamie and the Hebrew War." Bernadette's mother, a television newswoman, adopts a four-year-old Vietnamese orphan, to whom Bernadette enjoys teaching English.

A Honey of a Chimp is an unusual animal story. Thirteen-year-old Emily wants a pet, unlike a hamster or a fish, with whom she can establish a relationship. Her father is allergic to cats, however, and her mother dislikes dogs. The family finally settles on a baby female pygmy chimpanzee. When the pet, called Olivia, becomes too mature to keep peacefully in a New York apartment, Emily is persuaded to donate her to the well-equipped San Diego Zoo. Emily decides that she will make chimpanzees her life's work, envisioning herself as a sort of Jane Goodall. In addition to her parents, Emily has an affectionate uncle; the family accepts his being gay and his employment as a gourmet cook for a wealthy family.

Robbie and the Leap Year Blues is the less interesting account of Robbie, an eleven-year-old New Yorker who divides his time between the apartments of his divorced parents. At his school there is a leap year day, during which a girl who admires him asks Robbie to be her husband in mock marriage ceremonies. A delightful Armenian baby named Tigran, called "Tiger," is brought into the school to help teach the students child care skills. Though Robbie has not caught up with the girls in psychosexual development, he especially enjoys caring for Tigran, who wins the part of the Baby Jesus in the school pageant.

A final book designed chiefly for children is *Baryshnikov's Nutcracker* (1983), in which Klein accepted the difficult challenge of retelling the story of a favorite ballet, without the benefit of motion and music. Supporting her words is only a collection of undistinguished photographs of the American Ballet Theatre production, with choreography by Baryshnikov. The book is nevertheless pleasing, because Klein's narrative does manage to convey some of the romantic enchantment of the ballet: the Christmas wonder of toy soldiers, frosted windows, talking animals, and fairyland princes. Klein succeeds in conveying the wonder of what the dust jacket aptly refers to as "that last mystical moment before a young girl becomes a woman."

Klein's books for young children are a prime example of the range of her sympathies and her versatility. They are all competently constructed and have more than an average amount of charm, wit, and insight. Children's books, rightly or wrongly, tend to be highly didactic. Klein's books present their lessons with more subtlety than most and with messages more seamlessly integrated into the plot structures.

3. Young Adult Fiction: "Strong, Interesting People"

Klein has called herself a midlist writer of adult fiction rather than a best-selling author.[1] She may indeed be in the midlists when she writes for children or adults, but when she writes for teenagers she becomes a superstar. In the young adult field her name recognition is enormous with young readers, their teachers, librarians, and book dealers. Perhaps only Judy Blume has a more devoted following.

The classification of Klein's books has been especially problematic when she has written about teenagers. The perplexity belongs more to her publishers than to her readers, however; the latter tend to be quite clear about what they like. Several of Klein's books about teenagers have been published as adult fiction; fearing protests from education and parent organizations, publishers have found it safer to publish these books on the adult lists. This has been especially true when the book has been even more open than usual about sexual matters or of greater length than is normally considered desirable for young people. Nevertheless, Klein recognizes that the proper audience has generally found her books, even when readers have been forced to search a little harder to locate them on the shelves of libraries and book stores.

Klein's stated desire has been to write young adult books in which the central characters are "strong, interesting people" working bravely through the conflicts and problems that especially afflict persons their age.[2] Though her first books were about girls, and always conveyed a message of feminist uplift, she was not long in discovering that boys too need strong, interesting literary models. While any young adult novel by Klein will provide examples of characters who demonstrate strength, if not exceptional heroism, five narratives in particular, written over a period of twelve years, should be sufficient to establish that the stated goal has been largely achieved.

It's Not What You Expect was published in 1973. Though it is not one of the more frequently discussed of Klein's novels, it has many interesting features and two especially notable characters. The central protagonists are Oliver and Carla Simon, fourteen-year-old twins, who show greater maturity than their age would suggest. During a crucial summer they must cope with major family problems while they creatively and successfully establish a business enterprise. Oliver is a talented gourmet cook who, with Carla's encouragement and help, decides to open a summer restaurant in a house the twins have been given the responsibility of caretaking. Carla will be the maitress d'hôte, while Oliver will be the principal chef. Their menu, simple but delicious, will feature a single meal each evening which will sell for eight dollars a plate. As a tribute to Marcel Proust, a writer whose *Du côté de chez Swann* the precocious Carla especially admires, they call their restaurant A Côté de Chez Simon. They staff it with family members and people they date. An immediate success, the venture makes money, and all participants enjoy its operation. Klein provides enough details of restaurant management and menus to give her narrative verisimilitude and interest. The young reader actually savors the vicarious experience of setting up and conducting the daily activities of a restaurant.

Family complications, however, mar the happiness of an otherwise successful summer. Dad, who rather curiously looks like both George C. Scott and Albert Camus, decides family responsibilities have prevented him from writing a successful novel. He leaves home, grows a beard, and affects a trenchcoat similar to that worn by his idol Camus. Renting a "bachelor pad" in New

York City, he is soon joined by a girlfriend, a music professor whom the children find most unmistresslike in appearance. More perceptive and secure than most wives would be, Mother happens to understand Dad's midlife crisis, remembering that he—unlike herself, a native New Yorker—grew up in a small midwestern town. She believes that after he has his fling Dad will return to the family and his stable if prosaic job as a psychological counselor for a small college. Mom has amorous complications of her own, but she resists the opportunity to get even with Dad, rejecting the advances of a neighbor who has long been infatuated with her.

Older brother Tom presents the most serious problem to ruffle the smooth flow of summer. His girlfriend, a real "cupcake" named Sara Lee, becomes pregnant. Because she and Tom have been sweethearts since third grade, without complications, this family emergency was not anticipated. When Oliver and Carla generously offer to donate the proceeds of their restaurant to pay for Sara Lee's abortion, Tom becomes angrily defensive, insisting that he can finance his own girlfriend's abortions.

With such crises the summer becomes a period of self-discovery for everyone. It is Carla, most of all, who reaches a measure of self-understanding. An intelligent, forceful young woman, she comes to admit that there is some truth in the description others often give of her as self-righteous. With her own life in relative order, she has been quick to judge the other members of her family in their escapades. First she examined Dad's bachelor apartment disapprovingly, found his novel tedious, and pronounced his girlfriend unattractive. She admits to snooping and eavesdropping. She has also been so quick to judge Tom and Sara Lee that his indignant response to her offer of money is not surprising. Yet Carla is able to develop compassion, particularly after Mom, whom she admires, produces a surprising revelation of her own youth. Mom admits that she too had an abortion, after a sad, early love affair.

The novel ends with one of Norma Klein's justly celebrated dinner scenes, this time a large communal family meal held during the last night of the season at Chez Simon. All members of the family, now reunited, have learned the perhaps trite but no less real lesson that life is not exactly "what you expect." They have come to new understandings of one another, the children in particular acknowledging that they must be less demanding in their expectations of their parents. Family loyalty is reaffirmed.

Though abortion even thirteen years ago was not as readily accepted a topic in young adult fiction as it is today, the novel did not attract as much attention as might have been expected. Perhaps most readers found it static and a trifle too intellectual, with its allusions to Proust and its descriptions of gourmet meals. It is also one of Klein's few novels in which economics is a serious ingredient. Readers may have had difficulty responding to these features. Yet there was much of the author's familiar charm in the narrative, particularly in the account of youthful enterprise and the characterization of Carla as forceful and interesting, if a mite too judgmental and unyielding. The book was also strongly pro-family, its happy ending almost Hollywood-style, with the family back together at Côté de Chez Simon.

Bizou, published in 1983, is one of those thin novels that Norma Klein describes as having "vanished without a trace." Yet it has not been entirely ignored; it was noted by the *Horn Book* upon publication and has recently reappeared in paperback. In fact, it has had some success in the latter edition. Recent paperback advertising of subsequent books has even started identifying Klein as "the author of *Bizou.*" The first critics, however, pointed out the narrative's rather obvious flaws. *Publisher's Weekly* found the book "slangy and sloppy," lacking adequate motivations for the actions of the central characters, which the reviewer described as "two-dimensional people who never develop." The story was declared "simplistic, unresolved and trivial."[3] While *Horn Book* recommended it for ages twelve and up and saw some skill in the narrative structure, the reviewer found the denouement "disappointing."[4] Anne Connor in *School Library Journal* observed that the book's fast pace would attract readers unconcerned with stylistic finesse but that the characters were too shallow and the plot too unrealistic. Issues of racism and child abandonment, which should have made the story timely, were not dealt with in any "significant" manner, she concluded.[5]

The two central figures in *Bizou,* a mother and daughter, are black. Though the characterizations are, on the whole, successful, Klein has acknowledged some limitations when she has written about blacks. She has not written about racial interactions very much and has no plans to do so in the future, regarding the subject as "too fraught."[6] Her own acquaintance with black people has not been broad but confined largely to the urban, upwardly mobile, if street-smart friends of her younger daughter. Klein took the germ of the plot of *Bizou* not from firsthand observation of black people but from a movie about a German woman who temporarily left her child in the care of a stranger. The racial complications were simply added.

Despite the noticeable flaws that critics quickly identified, the novel has some interesting features. A glamorous American black woman, ironically named Tranquillity, has made a career in French high fashion. She is now the widow of a French-Jewish photographer, who was a hero of the Resistance. Initially, Tranquillity is well drawn, her insecurities believable. Her ambivalences about her native land are also convincing. A success in France, she is apprehensive about returning to her own country for the first time in many years but wishes her daughter to know something of family origins. The daughter, Bizou—which is French for "little kiss"—is a lively, intelligent teenager of European education and style. Arriving in the United States for the first time, she has a natural curiosity about her American relatives.

During the trans-Atlantic flight, Tranquillity makes friends with a young Jewish-American medical student who reminds her of her deceased husband. While the three are exploring New York City together, Tranquillity reacts to a racist-sexist slur she receives in a shop by disappearing. She leaves Bizou in the care of the young man, even though she knows he is anxious to get back to his university and does not need to be hindered by the custody of a foreign child. Tranquillity's desertion of her child in a strange land—though she does leave behind plenty of money and a semi-explanatory letter—is not credible, especially since the reader has been made to believe she is a solid citizen.

When the American relatives are finally introduced, late in the book, the novel becomes even harder to accept, and a trite, moralistic ending almost spoils a narrative that started with much promise. Tranquillity's father turns out to be an elderly doctor, so refined and saintly that it is difficult to understand why his daughter ever fled to Europe to escape his influence. An earlier child, whom Tranquillity had deserted even before her first departure for France, also turns up. Abandonment, it seems, is not a new strategy for Tranquillity.

Unfortunately, the book does not further explore the psychology of the black woman, and her relatives, when belatedly introduced, turn out to be cardboard bores. Her story could have been much more interesting, because Klein initially captured with effectiveness the feelings of this beautiful woman, acclaimed in France as an exotic beauty, who returns to America where she is regarded as "just another Negra."

Klein gives Bizou more consistency. A vastly more responsible person than her mother, she copes well with her abandonment in a crime-ridden city of a foreign land. She immediately starts making her survival plans, mentally listing the Americans she has met in France. Contending with adolescent infatuation, in the midst of her other problems, she does not fail to contact the American boyfriend she had known earlier in France.

After being eventually reunited with her mother and finding herself unable to express resentment directly, Bizou jumps off the roof in protest, breaking her leg. Her statement is heard, its message understood even by the self-absorbed Tranquillity. When Bizou finally returns with her mother to France, a place where they decide they unquestionably belong, she promises to keep in touch with the relatives and many friends she has found in America. She has truly made the best of the difficult situation into which she was thrust, and the reader knows that Bizou, unlike her irresponsible mother, will always be able to face difficult situations in the future rather than run away from them.

As first-person narrator, Bizou is revealed from the beginning to be intelligent and thoughtful. Though she is not openly judgmental of her mother, it is evident that tension has been mounting when she jumps off the roof. Tranquillity, even though she is the parent, is a much less self-realized individual than her daughter. Commitment is difficult for her. Though she has lived in an environment of artists and models, her life has been relatively circumspect. There have certainly been boyfriends, including one who "lived in" for a year, yet she seems not to have been seriously involved with a man since the death of her husband. Bizou appears immune to the titillation of interracial sex, unlike several of the other characters. Her mother has taught her that sexual relationships are all right if she feels she can handle them. Mother's motto throughout seems to be: do what you can, if you can handle the situation. Often, however, Tranquillity cannot really cope; she makes quick judgments and acts without reflection. Bizou is not like this. She is, in fact, the necessary steadying influence on her mother.

The earlier narratives on which Klein made her reputation were centered around the experiences of teenage women. More recently she has discovered the advantages of writing from the young male point of view, expanding—at least theoretically—her market to include the broader base of readers of fiction about young men. The majority of the young adult novels of the last few years, which have included some of Klein's finest writing, have developed around interesting and strong young male protagonists who tell their own stories.

Snapshots, published in 1984, is a highly moral book in message and direction. It treats the problem of child pornography, or more precisely the pathological fear of the sex appeal that a young child may exert on older persons. *Snapshots* is the story of two friends, Marc and Sean, who are skilled amateur photographers. They decide that Marc's little sister, Tiffany, would be a terrific model. Though she is only eight years old, she is an extraordinarily beautiful little girl, well aware of her charm, who poses naturally before a camera. Since they think of her as a child, they have no hesitancy in making nude photographs of her, which they regard as classic baby pictures. Yet someone working on their film in the developing laboratory interprets the pictures in a very different light. The district attorney's office is alerted, and the two boys are accused of manufacturing child pornography. Sean and Marc soon discover that they are in genuine trouble. Though their families hire lawyers to defend them, even their fathers start questioning their motives.

Sean, who is the first-person narrator, is an especially interesting and likable character. Though he does not come from a religious family, he is learning Hebrew and preparing for his bar mitzvah. His family, while Jewish by ethnic heritage, must make haste to join a synagogue so that he will have a place for his bar mitzvah ceremony. While Sean cannot fully articulate his reasons for wanting the traditional service, the reader readily understands his desire to attach himself to an ancient and profound tradition which, by birth if not by family training, is his due.

Sean makes an effort to explain why he is preparing for his bar mitzvah: "I thought it would be fun and it would give me some sense of my roots. I didn't go through any profound religious experience, but I think it's the kind of thing that once I've done it, I'll be glad I did."

His sister, a feminist, sees the bar mitzvah as an occasion for making a social statement. Though she personally feels that "a bar mitzvah in a Reform synagogue followed by a banquet in a Chinese restaurant is the last word in nothing," and that Judaism is a sexist religion, she argues that Sean should at least use a woman rabbi. He is quite willing, especially when he discovers that his sister's new boyfriend, a weird-looking, long-haired type, happens to have a rabbinical sister. Though their father resents having feminism injected into every family discussion and claims he will "go crazy" if he has to listen to another women's rights lecture, he too agrees, perceiving even in his dimly secular way that a bar mitzvah is, whatever else it represents, a ceremony of family togetherness.

Sean has a serious discussion about his approaching bar mitzvah with Joanie, his gentile girlfriend:

> "Are you Jewish?" Joanie asked.
> "Yeah. That's how come I'm doing this."

"Are your parents religious?"

"Not that much." I told her about how Marsha wanted a woman rabbi to do the ceremony.

"Can they be women?" Joanie asked. "I thought they had to be men and wear those little hats and everything."

"No, they can be women," I explained, "but it's more rare. And my father thinks it's strange. He thinks my sister is too much of a feminist."

"I wouldn't want to be a rabbi or a priest or anything like that," Joanie said. "Sometimes I'm not even sure if I believe in God!"

"Me too," I said. "I'm not sure what I believe yet."

"You don't have to believe in anything," Joanie said. "But you can STILL BE A GOOD PERSON AND ALL THAT."

"Sure," I said. "I hope I'm a good person. Sometimes I'm not that sure."

Having this discussion, he discovers, makes him lose interest in "making out" with his girlfriend, but he is delighted that she is understanding. It is usually hard for him to have such serious discussions. He is not able to tell his parents that he is not sure he believes in God, because he fears he would then have to explain to them why he wants the bar mitzvah in the first place.

Despite his crotchety conversation and demeanor, Sean's father is totally supportive of him in his problems with the D.A. Explanations are finally accepted, and the matter of the questionable photographs is resolved. Sean's father even brings himself to admit that the pictures are of professional quality and that Tiffany Campbell is "one sexy little girl." He confides that he is glad she is not his, considering the trouble Mr. Campbell is likely to have with her many suitors in a few years. Sean reassures Dad that he will never have that problem with his own chubby, argumentative sister Marsha!

The bar mitzvah turns out to be a big occasion for the entire family and their Jewish and gentile friends. Father makes a speech praising his son's maturity and dignity throughout his recent crisis. Sean composes and delivers his own speech, expressing his gratitude for the support of his family. He concludes by affirming that he will always remember that he is part of an ancient tradition, with the responsibility of preserving it. As he reads his ceremonial Hebrew, which he does not fully understand even as he recites it, he willingly accepts the responsibilities of Jewish manhood. The ceremony has also sealed the unity of even this secular family.

Give and Take, published in 1985, has presented a special problem in classification, and might best be called a "mature young adult novel." It is a very funny narrative that deserves to be dramatized, perhaps as a television movie. Because of its sensitive, if highly humorous, central situation, it was published on the adult lists, although Klein obviously intended it for her youth readership. The publisher liked the book from its first submission and agreed to publish it as a young adult novel, provided Klein changed the summer occupation of her hero-narrator. She wisely refused to comply with this request, because the change would have destroyed much of the fun of the narrative and demolished its central point.

Give and Take is not only a strong example of Klein's increasing use of the young male as protagonist and first-person narrator, but it provides further evidence of her fondness for choosing older protagonists as her own daughters have approached the end of their teen years. The central characters of the book are caught up in the bittersweet days of their last summer before college. Spence, the narrator, is a bright eighteen-year-old who remains an innocent, though he is constantly pursued by women who want to seduce him. One of them, Taffy, is obsessed with possessing him, even though she was a shotgun bride only a few months ago and is already a mother. Spence resists seduction, probably because of his shyness, but also because he insists that he must have affection and concern for a woman before he has sex with her. A further reason for avoiding sex is his summer job as donor at the local sperm bank clinic. Taking his work very seriously, he has agreed to keep his sperm count high, abstaining from all sexual relations. He is conscientious at keeping promises and regards himself as a philanthropist who is making an outstanding contribution to the human race, particularly to the happiness of countless unseen women who would not otherwise be able to become mothers. Although Spence has good intentions, the women who lust after him lay many traps, and he does not totally manage to escape their snares.

Klein, who admits that the titles of her books have sometimes been dreadful, originally intended to call the book *The Donor.* Unfortunately, she allowed herself to be talked into changing the title, in order to avoid calling undue attention to Spence's vocation in the sperm bank, though it was, in fact, the main point of the narrative. Klein says she got this very funny and creative concept by reading some years back in the *New York Times,* or perhaps it was *Mother Jones,* about sperm banks and an unnamed young man in his twenties who led a lonely life but was a dedicated donor at his local sperm bank. The plot developed from the image of this young man, a virgin and shy with women, who felt a mission to vicariously impregnate.

It may be significant that Spence is an orphan who has been reared by his grandparents, kindly if eccentric people. When his grandfather dies, Spence again reveals his strong sense of responsibility. He takes his grandmother to the lake to sprinkle Grandfather's ashes and reads an A. E. Housman poem Grandfather is supposed to have liked. He is also able to deal compassionately with Grandmother's strange behavior when she later takes out an old photo of Grandfather, places it in a chair, and starts conversing with it. Taffy, a certifiable psychotic who finally has to be committed, has no trouble sharing Grandmother's fantasy, and Spence must deal gently with both of them.

Although the complications in Spence's personal life, Grandmother's grief, and Taffy's mental illness, hinder his success during his first semester at Michigan State, he appears to be pulling himself together by the end of the book. He seems certain to do well in his premed studies. Not only has he demonstrated moral strength through crisis, but he has shown that he can be a determined and steady young man.

Give and Take introduces well-conceived characters, though Klein is out of her usual New York upper middle-class environment. The book's success suggests again the considerable range, not yet fully realized, that Klein potentially possesses. Her portrait of midwestern small-town life is convincing. There is genuine wit in the reversal of the usual male-female roles in courtship and seduction, as Spence must struggle against predatory women and find good excuses for his refusal to accept their propositions. When women approach him, this summer employee of a sperm donor bank usually pleads that he is afraid of begetting a child! On the whole, the book is upbeat, despite the mental aberrations of the grandmother and Taffy and the teen struggle for self-realization that is left uncompleted at the end. Spence is one of the funniest and most lovable characters to appear in recent young adult fiction.

In *The Cheerleader* (1985) Klein returned to the adventures of younger protagonists. The fourteen-year-old hero-narrator, Evan Siegal, lives with his older brother, his mother, and stepfather Harold, a whimsically eccentric individual whom he likes very much. His own father, to whom he relates less easily, lives in Florida. Dad is a former social worker who now operates a stereo shop. Once a year, during the month of both boys' birthdays, Dad comes to New York to visit them, and he dutifully calls them each week on the telephone. Though he tries to be solicitous, his sons find him trying and embarrassing in his melancholy habit of brooding over his bad fortune and the general sadness of the human situation. Dad's personality is, however, developed with a touch of Klein's gentle satire.

With its assortment of likable characters, this narrative of high school exploits is well sustained. Evan's serious-minded girl-friend, Laurie, thinks cheerleaders are all fools. Rachel, an empty-headed, bosomy cheerleader liked by Karim, Evan's best friend, seems to lend support to this thesis. Rachel, who is full of her own importance, is more interested in Evan himself, who—unlike his studious and musically talented older brother—is highly suc-cessful with girls. Though he is not above fantasizing about Rachel, Evan easily rejects her overtures when they come.

Karim is an equally interesting and attractive young man. While Evan is culturally Jewish, Karim is the son of an oil-rich Saudi Arabian. His mother, who comes from Texas, is a clothing designer who dresses her son in high fashion attire that makes him an object of ridicule at school. Karim also lives in a posh hotel and travels abroad extensively. Though he has no airs and is a gentle and sensitive person, his classmates treat him badly because he is obviously not one of them. They dismiss him as a rich foreigner with odd ways. Only Evan is devoted to him.

Evan decides, in the interests of sexual equality, that girls' sports need boys as cheerleaders. Karim, as usual, is ready to go along with him on any project. At first their new idea is laughed away by their classmates, but, with determination, they go ahead with their plan. They dress up like rock stars, in interesting costumes designed by Karim's mother, and are an immediate hit when they start performing at games. The younger girls even start a fan club, and both boys are mobbed by girls who want to give them phone numbers.

All the central characters in this teenage comedy fiction end up by "getting the girls." Karim finds a less glamorous but much nicer girlfriend than Rachel, one who truly appreciates his sensitivity. Even Evan's shy and brilliant older brother gets a date, through Evan's maneuvering.

While there is not much action, the book sustains interest largely through its two central personalities. The Jewish-Arab friendship is well handled, with understatement and without cant. It is Karim's father who is not too convincing, as a liberated Arab male who comes to live in the United States partly because he finds relationships between men and women are more open and free here. But it is Evan who stands out as one of the strongest, most creative, most liberated, and liberating of the characters that Klein has created. His imagination overflows with creative ideas. Like Huckleberry Finn and Holden Caulfield, he is a young man with a good heart, totally without guile.

Klein's works are populated with young men and women—along with their parents—who are caught up in the process of self-realization and self-discovery. They are striving to become stronger individuals, and most do succeed. More often than not, the young people succeed better than the adults. This is a literature, like most popular genres, that flatters its readers and provides reassurance as, in book after book, young people overcome obstacles and discover themselves. Klein might also, with some justice, be accused of accepting the doctrine of the 1960s that the young of the world are its saving remnant. Though she avoids most of the clichés of recent movements that have glorified youth at the expense of their elders, her young people are still more moral, more ethical, and much better company than most of their seniors.

4. The Central Quest: Sexuality and Love

Most of Norma Klein's books in both the young adult and adult categories show individuals, whatever else their interests, on a central quest, for sexuality and love. Life for persons of all ages, Klein would seem to be saying, is centered around this basic pursuit, yet this quest seems especially urgent and even poignant when the characters are teenagers. While one may experience sex without love, and discover some merit therein, love without sex is almost incomprehensible. Though sex and affection are best combined, a sexual relationship does not have to involve a pledge of undying love to be meaningful in the context of a Klein novel. The idealized love—earth shattering, spiritually exalting, and doomed—celebrated by the great poets of the Western World is absent from Klein's fictional universe. On the other hand, the expression of sexuality is always a part of the task of finding oneself, of making the bridge from childhood to the adult role.

While all the young adult novels feature sexuality and love as one focus, Klein's approach may best be examined in four particularly crucial novels dealing with teenagers who are discovering themselves, in good part through their sexuality. Three are original works, while the fourth is a fictionalization of a film.

It's OK If You Don't Love Me (1977), an original narrative, unfolds in the New York setting where the author is most comfortable. Jody, a typical Klein heroine-narrator, is a liberated young woman from a Jewish family. Her boyfriend Lyle, on the other hand, is a more straitlaced midwesterner from a Roman Catholic background. The two are caught up in an unlikely romance. Lyle, whose parents have recently been killed in an automobile accident, has come to New York to live in the modest apartment of his sister, her husband, and their infant child. A bright young man, the son of a college professor, Lyle is determined to make something of himself. Though he is accepted into Ivy League colleges, he chooses Haverford because it offers him both a program he wants and an almost complete scholarship. Jody is also accepted into top schools yet, to her mother's annoyance, chooses Swarthmore over Radcliffe for personal reasons that demonstrate substance over superficial glitter.

Jody's life-style differs radically from that which Lyle has always known. She lives in a New York apartment with her younger brother, her mother, and her mother's live-in boyfriend, Elliot, a psychiatrist. Jody still sees Phillip, her former stepfather, to whom she is deeply attached. He is described as a brilliant, eccentric scientist. Once a year she also dutifully makes a trip to see her real father, whom she thoroughly dislikes. He is a prosperous dentist, well established in the suburbs. Her stepmother, Boots, makes an effort to be pleasant, despite Jody's antipathy. There are two half-sisters who are well characterized; while the younger tries to be Jody's friend, the older is thoroughly unpleasant. In describing this assortment of people, Klein succeeds in drawing a convincing picture of contemporary family life among the divorced upper middle classes.

Despite great differences in background—probably because of these very differences—Jody and Lyle fall in love. Jody is the aggressor, and it takes her a while to seduce the almost unbelievably reticent Lyle. She is not inexperienced in matters sexual; even before her big romance with Lyle, she had a lover, her old school chum Whitney. When Whitney returns for a visit to their school she has a final assignation with him, which, not surprisingly, leads to a quarrel and estrangement from Lyle.

Mom also has a fight with Elliot, repeating in a minor key the problems in the life of her daughter. The plot, with its string of misunderstandings and assorted couplings, reads a bit like a Renaissance comedy, and that is the way it ends, with even the unlikely characters paired off with mates. Jody, by implication, is back with Lyle; little brother Eric acquires a girlfriend; Mother makes up with Elliot; and even stepfather Phillip, an unlikely mate for anyone, allows a woman to move into his apartment. Klein's books usually end happily, and this one is no exception; all that is lacking at the end is Mendelssohn music and the blessing of the Fairy Queen.

The book introduces several minor themes. Jody's dentist father is held up as the doleful end product of the aspirations of aggressive Jewish mothers for their sons, of vulgar materialism out of control. He insists on taking his son Eric, who is totally disinterested, to sporting events. On Eric's sixteenth birthday Dad insensitively suggests introducing him to a really good call girl. Eric is insulted, and Mom, who has long had Dad's number, is furious when she learns of his intentions.

Lyle's family reflects the values of gentile non-New Yorkers, in conflict with those of Jody's family, city residents. His sister and brother-in-law, though well-meaning, have their stereotyped notions of New Yorkers, especially of Jewish girls bred in the city. They politely try to talk to Jody about Israel, though it soon becomes evident that she has neither religious interests nor ethnic identifications. Later her conversation with Lyle's sister on abortion points up another conflict. The sister, in character with her Roman Catholic upbringing, regards abortion as murder, while Jody considers it a valid medical procedure. Not surprisingly, Jody finds Lyle's sister judgmental and self-righteous. The alleged number of broken homes found among "Jewish kids" is another area of disapproval for the sister. In New York everyone seems to be "confessing" to a psychiatrist, she observes. She labels this another instance of muddled secularism.

Jody's own notions of small-town midwestern life come right out of fiction rather than experience or any real understanding of human nature. To her, small-town America is simultaneously backward and sexually advantageous. "I have the feeling he might have had quite a lot of sexual experience. [She thinks of Lyle] People do in small towns, according to some of the books I've read. There just isn't much else to do. The other thing is that in small towns teenagers go around in cars most of the time, unlike the city, where we tend to go by subway or bus. And so their idea of a date is to park in some dark field and screw in the back seat of the car."

While Jody feels that Lyle is "riddled with Middle American prejudices," Lyle has difficulty coming to terms with the New York ethos. He feels city relationships are shallow, and urban conduct often thoughtless. He says of Jody's sexual betrayal with Whitney: "Well, sorry. I guess I'm not a liberated, swinging New Yorker yet, but it strikes me as pretty damn inexcusable." Jody regards herself as an urbane feminist, and thinks she is fortunate in having good role models of liberated women. Her mother has a successful career in a literary agency—though she is somewhat less successful in marriage—and Jody looks forward to being equally independent financially, whether or not she marries. At one point she speculates that it would be interesting if either male or female could become pregnant in a relationship. To further complicate the situation, she feels that it would be only fair if a couple could never know which one at a given point might be tapped for the childbearing role. Lyle is, predictably, more comfortable with human biology and traditional sex role expectations.

Much of Jody's thinking centers on sex, not unlike many others her age, in fiction or real life. Her philosophy is that if she likes someone well enough to kiss him, why not do the rest. She does not, however, think of herself as promiscuous, and she does have the grace to feel guilty about her betrayal of Lyle with Whitney. Relationships do, after all, mean something in this book: loyalty and trust are not outdated virtues, though chastity may be. Her motives in sleeping again with Whitney, she recognizes, were not the best. She wanted to show him her better figure and improved sexual performance, after her considerable experience with Lyle.

Lyle is much more hesitant about sex, though he allows Jody to entice him. There is some frank discussion of sexual performance, and both young people agree that men and women make too much out of a woman's sexual climaxing. Jody, despite her liberated attitudes, is slow in achieving sexual completion. In fact, she does not have a sexual climax with Lyle until immediately after they have devastatingly defeated her father and his friend at tennis doubles. This ultimate sexual experience also, significantly, takes place in the bathroom at her Dad's place. Norma Klein's Freudian psychology is, as always, clearly in place.

It's OK If You Don't Love Me, which is even more frank about sexuality than Klein's previous young adult books and contains more details of the physiology of sex, was published on the adult lists, despite its more obvious appeal to teenagers. It is one of several Klein books that publishers felt might raise the ire of school officials if recommended for the young adult shelves of libraries and bookstores. In sum, it is an interest-sustaining but unexceptional story of the attraction of opposites, of feminist conflicts, regional clashes, and of the new morality set face-to-face with traditional values. Needless to say, the new standards of sexuality and the New York ethos win out. Klein's publishers may have been right in gauging the likely response in the provinces.

Beginner's Love, published in 1983, is another adolescent romance, this time with a young male narrator named Joel. The principals are again the rather customary assortment of New Yorkers that readers have come to expect in a Klein novel. Joel's mother operates an art gallery, while his father is a restaurant reviewer and writer on gourmet foods. Both parents are colorful individuals. Joel meets Leda, an attractive young woman with equally flamboyant parents. Her mother is an actress, and her father manages a theatre. Joel and Leda are soon absorbed in an ardent love affair. Though they profess undying love, their relationship does not survive Leda's abortion, even though they both decide to attend Yale and there is no pressing reason for them to separate.

Too many events and attitudes are never explained. Despite the ardor of his affair with Leda at its peak, Joel, in the end, seems to prefer his former girlfriend Lassie, and the reader is never clear exactly why. Despite all Leda's beliefs about worry-free abortion, her own is a genuine crisis that seems to destroy her relationship with Joel. Again, the reader never really knows why this liberated woman, from an unconventional family, should find a legally and socially approved medical procedure so traumatic. If subterranean currents exist in these characters, the reader is given no clear indication of them until unexpected choices are made, seemingly without provocation.

Despite problems in the narrative, Klein's humor does not fail and is noticeably evident in the minor characters. Joel has a brother who is a rich West Coast dental surgeon—dentistry in Klein's writing always signals bourgeois values at their lowest—who marries during the course of the book. When the family goes out to the Coast for the wedding, they meet the new daughter-in-law. Persons frequently have unexpected professions in Klein books, and this bride turns out to be a successful funeral director.

An interesting bit of literary criticism of young adult fiction is made quite unobtrusively by the characters in this book. In the middle of coping with their abortion problem, Leda and Joel find themselves discussing books for teenagers, obviously the sort of books Norma Klein does not write. These are books in which a young couple has to get married, the girl drops out of school to take care of the baby, and the two live over a garage where the boy works on used cars. There is always some scene where another girl who has had an abortion comes to visit and is discovered to be approaching insanity or ready to become a Bowery bum. Leda and Joel have probably been reading *Mr. and Mrs. Bo Jo Jones,* a novel by Ann Head that was much discussed in the late sixties and early seventies.

Leda observes:

> every other book I've read since I was *ten* is like that. The girl's a moron, the guy's a moron, they never heard of birth control. What I love are the scenes where the father takes the guy aside and says, "Son, if you marry Betsy, you'll have to give up your football scholarship to Oklahoma State." They're *always* going to some godforsaken place like Oklahoma State! And the guy says, "But, Dad I love her! . . . And then there's a scene where

the mother says, "Dear, you haven't let him take advantage of
you? You know what boys are like." Quote unquote. . . . God
I think writers must be really dumb! Or else they're living in
the Stone Age.

Though these words are placed in the mouth of a youthful character, it is hard to avoid the conclusion that they also express
Klein's feelings about much of her competition. Many of the people
who have written books about teenage problems have in her judgment written them badly.

One of Klein's tasks in this book is obvious; today with legal
and socially acceptable abortion, it is difficult to make an un-
anticipated teen pregnancy dramatic and suspenseful, especially
when it occurs in a liberal middle-class environment. Perhaps the
one way out of the possible tedium of the situation is to satirize
the approaches of the past, along with the attitudes of people for
whom Oklahoma State would represent advancement and culture. The all-too-familiar element of regional snobbery seems here
to come not merely from the characters but from their author as
well.

Despite its male narrator, *Beginner's Love* is probably of primary interest to female readers in grades ten through twelve.
Klein's understanding of teen fashions, fads, current films, and
rock stars—perhaps because she has listened well to her daughters—is evident in the authenticity of detail in this book, even if
the reader is left a little confused by the way the characters cope
with the abortion and other major choices they must make.

Obviously flawed and repetitive within the Klein canon, the
book was not especially admired by reviewers. *School Library
Journal* said that the first-person narration could best be described as "first-person ramble." The dialogue was, somewhat
condescendingly, found to be "Valley Girl Talk," the reflections
"long-winded and tiresome." Lois A. Strell, who reviewed the
book, also concluded that the narrative was too saturated with
sex. She found that the characters generated little interest because their feelings were so shallow.[1] Kevin Kenny, who reviewed
the book for *Voice of Youth Advocates,* disagreed however, finding
the explicitness, the very frankness in matters sexual, thought-

provoking. Joel's musings on sex were, he felt, especially appropriate to a young man of the hero's age. The minor characters, so often a needless complication awkwardly integrated into youth novels, were, rightfully, pronounced pleasing and interesting. Kenny found only Leda to be a less than thoroughly believable character. It also took no special clairvoyance for Kenny to predict that the explicitness he praised would bring controversy as well as popularity to the book.[2]

French Postcards (1979), perhaps because it was a novelization of a movie with a Parisian setting not very familiar to the author, is one of Klein's weakest books, however interesting its exploration of teenage sexuality might well have been. It appears to have been hastily written to cash in on modest interest generated by a motion picture. The action is chaotic and not too clearly motivated at several points. At the end of the book almost all the characters are frantically tumbling into various beds. Paris, so central to the sense of the plot, is only vaguely realized as a setting. Because they are so inadequately individualized, the characters also never truly capture the reader's imagination.

Yet the plot presents real possibilities—situations more or less thrown away—that Klein might well return to at her artistic leisure. Four young Americans are spending their junior year abroad at an institution operated by a glamorous thirty-five-year-old French woman, Madame Tessier, and her older, rather cranky husband. Madame Tessier follows the familiar Continental tradition (which exists widely in literature though no one knows how widely in life) of initiating a young man into the joys of *l'amour*. Alex is her easy prey; he becomes infatuated with her, shadowing her in shops and on the streets. While pretending to be an innocent and somewhat misunderstood matron, she lures him to her luxurious house for an assignation. Her design, however, seems to be to prove a few points to her husband, who shows up unexpectedly and not surprisingly creates a scene.

It is never quite clear what Madame's full intentions are. Later her husband goes away, and her relationship with him remains ambiguous. She gives Alex an undeserved *A* in her class and offers him a job as her assistant for the next term. He refuses with some anger, obviously feeling he has been used.

Joel, another of the Americans, meets Toni, a French flutist who sleeps around much the way Americans expect French youth to do. They start an ardent affair, which ends with his bringing her back to the United States for marriage. Their view of marriage is considerably less than sacramental; realizing the problems of such international unions, they agree that there will be an easy divorce if their difficulties prove too complex to be worked out.

Susan, one of the American girls, sleeps with as many attractive French men as come her way. She believes this is what a young person in Paris is supposed to do. Her friend Laura, on the other hand, at first tries to be loyal to her boyfriend back home before finally surrendering to the Parisian mood and her desire to comfort Alex after his romantic mishaps with Madame Tessier.

All these young people—and perhaps their author as well—appear to have stereotyped notions of French courtship and sexuality, yet no truly significant cross-cultural observations are made. Consequently, the book seems pointless and ineffectual. As a fictionalization, *French Postcards* is much less successful than Klein's Sunshine books, which are on the whole quite strong. Though a forgettable book, *French Postcards,* like all Klein's fiction, is still readable. For verisimilitude it needs more detail, especially a greater feel for the city of Paris, which is, after all, so central to the book's mood of love madness. Nevertheless, despite its static quality, its poor realization of locale, and its ambiguous motivations, *French Postcards* was not a total critical failure. The reviewer for *Publisher's Weekly* felt "the story offers an entertaining insight into the traumas and triumphs of young love. Once again, Klein proves that this is a subject she handles deftly."[3]

Domestic Arrangements, published in 1981, is another of those novels that publishers had some difficulty classifying. Though too long and too bold to be placed in the young adult category, its subject matter, again, is obviously of most interest to that age group. The central character and narrator, Tatiana, is a Brooke

Shields clone, though Klein insists the character was based on the less well-known daughter of a personal acquaintance. During the course of discovering her own sexuality, Tatiana learns that her parents are both in love with others and will be getting a divorce. Yet this is no devastating discovery. Everyone decides to be civilized and remain on good terms, illustrating another Klein doctrine: just because a marriage breaks up does not mean it has been a failure. People change. They stop loving each other and move on to other attachments.

Though much is said in the novel about sex as the expression of genuine caring, the reader is left with the feeling that sex is valued by these characters chiefly for its pleasurable sensations. The novel seems to promote the greatly oversimplified view that sex is good for teenagers, if they are responsible. Responsibility is defined as having sex because one wants to and cares about the partner as a person. Tatiana gets a diaphragm from her parents as a Christmas present, though her father remains sceptical about her relationship with her boyfriend Joshua. Her sister also blithely begins an affair with Joshua's older brother, thus keeping much of the sexual activity within the same family.

Not all the sexual activity in this book is straight. Tatiana's co-star in her movie is gay; Joshua's former girlfriend has also come out of the lesbian closet; and good relationships exist between the gay and straight characters. In fact, they go out on double dates.

Another message of the narrative is that each person has to decide what is best for himself or herself. One should not live for others or simply to achieve wealth or fame. Tatiana turns down a two-hundred-thousand-dollar major motion picture role as the leading character in the musical version of *Lolita,* because she does not want to go to California or leave her school. Anyhow, she wants to be an obstetrician rather than an actress. There is, however, no indication in the narrative of any aptitude for a medical vocation.

Tatiana faces a genuine crisis with her self-image. Tired of hearing everyone talk about her striking beauty, she finally cuts her splendid mane of red hair as a protest. An important part of her crisis of self-image is the controversial nude scene in her film. It attracts much media attention as well as family concern. Dad especially, who has a bit of a fixation on Tatiana, is irate when he learns of it. Ultimately she rejects being a sex or beauty object and moves toward becoming more fully her own person. No doubt her rejection of all the usual glamour girl career choices is a major part of her new self-assertion. She is determined to make a contribution in an area that has nothing to do with physical beauty, however vaguely defined her specific goals may be.

Since *Domestic Arrangements* was another explicit coming-of-age story in the postsexual revolutionary United States, most reviewers observed that Klein had again presented classification problems for librarians, who would once more have to mobilize their arguments of redeeming social value for a book that looked like an adventure in "teenage wish-fulfillment."[4] All reviewers acknowledged, nevertheless, Klein's usual skill with dialogue, her considerable descriptive powers, her witty view of contemporary New Yorkers, and the story's general lack of pretentions.[5]

As usual, Klein's satirical skills served her well in *Domestic Arrangements,* especially in the scene where Tatiana, a juvenile sex symbol in the media and an example of postsexual revolutionary innocence, naively announces on a television talk show that she has asked her father for a diaphragm as a Christmas present. The juxtaposition of the still rather leering adult view of sex and the modern teenager's openness is amusingly presented.

Though everyone, young or old, seems in pursuit of sex and/or love, with varying degrees of franticness, Klein's treatment of sex never becomes salacious. Even if she wished, it is highly doubtful that she could be a skilled pornographic writer. Her view of sexuality lacks the perverse seriousness required for such an endeavor. Neither is she a romantic writer; sex in her books is not smothered in roses and music. It is an act that is pleasurable but hardly the quasi-religious experience that it becomes in romantic writing. Klein usually does not linger over the biological details of sexual encounters, perhaps realizing that there is only so much that can be said and that it has already been said many times over in countless popular novels. Neither does sexuality in Klein books have a dark side; it never brings grief or death. There are no Tristans or Isoldes in Norma Klein's New York City.

Her view of sexuality might be said to be comic above all else; there is, after all, something almost Chaplinesque about an entire fictional world composed of individuals madly pursuing one another, male after female, female after male, and even a minority of females and males after their own kind. If there is to be a criticism of Klein's treatment of sexuality, the accusation of flippancy rather than salaciousness might be more on the mark. Her young women lose their virginity without crisis, trauma, or even very much sense of adventure. Young men get seduced as much as they seduce, yet without the resonances that are found, for example, in those Continental novels that describe a youth's initiation into the pleasures of love under the tutelage of an overripe matron. Even the sexual experience that marks the boundary line between childhood and emerging adulthood often seems as much a matter of "getting on with it" as a ceremony of passage.

5. Feminism: Does God Look like Golda Meir?

In *It's OK If You Don't Love Me,* Jody, the first-person narrator, says to herself:

> I wonder what it'll be like if it turns out that there is a heaven after all and God, as I've always suspected, turns out to be a woman. I imagine She'll look like Golda Meir, stocky and wrinkled and wise, with kindly penetrating eyes. All the women in the world who thought of themselves as feminists will have to line up and take their turn justifying all the times they were ever crazily, dopily in love. I hope She will turn out to be a tennis player. Because, if I were talking about Lyle, I think I'd have to say, "If you saw his backhand, you'd understand." I hope that will make sense to Her.

Flippant though these lines are, they emphasize one of the leading ideas in Klein's work. Women's rights, Norma Klein believes, is the prime issue of the day, of more concern even than nuclear disarmament. (She lets her scientist husband demonstrate for that one. The problems of women are less abstract, more immediate.) Each day of her life, Klein believes, a woman is faced with unique problems. Even in her own highly sheltered life, where she works alone in her apartment and associates with friends of her own choosing, she feels that she has not fully escaped. As the mother of two intelligent and attractive daughters, she continues to worry that the lives of her children will be marred by the prejudices that restrict women. Looking at history, Klein sees discrimination fouling the lives of women of nearly every time and place.

What is to be done? For one thing, most feminists agree, books must be written that present strong female role models and healthy attitudes. Furthermore, a sisterhood united in resolve is essential.

While her books constantly promote the message of female liberation, Klein has still not been fully acknowledged as a leading advocate of women's rights. *Ms.,* though it has reviewed her juvenile books favorably, has never featured her and has not given her adult writings their due, while at the same time its editors and staff writers have praised the work of numerous women writers who are less gifted and effective. It does seem likely, as Klein has suggested herself, that the consistently positive portrayals of men in her writings may be one reason she has been suspect in the eyes of some radical feminists. Her strongly pro-family stance, in life and in art, may be another.

Though she allows considerable latitude in the expression of family loyalty, Klein's books have always been family stories. She does not tell us that the nuclear family is dead or that the freedom of women may be achieved only when all dependency upon males as lovers, husbands, or fathers has been renounced. While most feminists would not disagree with Klein's views, their emphasis has often tended to be on women striving to make it on their own without male support.

One sign of genuine sexual equality is a woman who is no longer a passive object of courtship. Klein's books frequently show young women as the aggressors in sexual relationships. These women are, furthermore, usually successful in their pursuit of the men they find desirable. In fact, Klein depicts women of all ages, especially grandmothers, striving for fulfillment not only in sexuality and family life but in creative and economic endeavors as well. An especially attractive Klein character is the lively grandmother, product of another era, who finds herself alone in late middle age, living comfortably on her deceased husband's money. Such a woman may take an interesting lover, develop a rich social life, and perhaps express herself in a business or an art. Although she has not publicly acknowledged it, in her portraits of the blooming older woman Klein may well have taken as a model her own gifted mother, the strikingly handsome Sadie Klein, who received her college degree in her seventies.

But not all Klein's fictional women are content and fulfilled. Some are matrons experiencing the pain of collapsing marriages, unequipped for gainful employment and psychologically unready for life alone. These women may be highly intelligent, with esoteric college diplomas (in Chinese poetry, for example, which may be Klein's fictional equivalent of her own expertise in Russian literature), who discover they have no marketable skills and feel themselves unwanted everywhere. A salary of thirty thousand dollars may become their frantic goal, their sad symbol of worldly success and even personal worth.

Though Klein's books show sympathy for the woman unhappily caught in a traditional role, it is usually the more competent and ambitious woman who succeeds. In *The Swap* and *Angel Face,* the educated or professionally skilled women not only have the more interesting lives but also win the affections of the desirable men. Whether or not such a pattern accurately reflects real life, it certainly violates the conventions of popular fiction, at least until recent decades, where men usually preferred the more clinging, dependent woman. This was especially true in books written for young people.

In *The Swap* (1983), another book for and about teenagers, though published on the adult lists, Maddy, an unassuming beautician and homemaker, loses the affections of her husband to lively, ambitious, and overprivileged Capri. It does not matter that Capri, who knows she is going places, has no permanent use for Maddy's husband; Capri is ready enough to dally with men along her way, if only for pleasure. Maddy remains a "sad sack" until she decides to take her life in hand, learning a trade that will provide more than a bare subsistence. In *Angel Face* (1984), the mother, though she has been an indifferent housekeeper and difficult spouse, feels greatly misused when her husband leaves her for a spinster social worker who has lived independently and earned her own living for many years. Klein obviously believes that the woman who is ambitious and successful in a career has more to offer a man in romance, companionship, and marriage.

At the same time, Klein can quickly quote the studies that seem to show that men are more comfortable with less educated, less sophisticated wives. If these studies are valid, there would seem to be little hope on the matrimonial market for the sort of young woman who is usually the heroine of her books, the high-achieving Ivy Leaguer. In her fictional contrasts between the lowly homebody who loses house, husband, and child and the bright, capable woman who reaches for it all, Klein is evidently presenting life as she feels it should be rather than as she fears it often is.

Nevertheless, Klein likes to show women demonstrating their independence in numerous ways. They pursue men, hold jobs, care for families, and express themselves artistically. They are their own persons. Symbolically, but significantly, they do not necessarily change their names when they marry. Ms. Korbel in *Angel Face* is a good example. There are many others. These women perform professional and occupational roles not normally associated with their sex in the popular mind. The women rabbis in the young adult books are especially pertinent and sometimes amusing examples. Klein consistently refuses to limit women to their traditional professional roles as teacher, nurse, or secretary. In fact, her women not only rarely practice the usual "women's professions," but they almost never appear in the socially unacceptable but no less traditional trades of women. There are no strippers or prostitutes in her books. Jobs that, though considered more honest, exploit women as sex objects are also not her favorite occupational choices for her characters. While a minority of her characters model fashions or appear on the stage, there are no stars of beauty pageants or cocktail hostesses.

Klein has never written a book that violated her feminist beliefs. In most of her narratives, in fact, she has managed to promote her sentiments in an active way. A closer look at two books that are typical in their presentation of women's concerns demonstrates the point.

The Queen of the What Ifs (1982) is a compassionate, realistic family narrative that presents several strong female characters of different ages. The story is told by Robin Vey, the fifteen-year-old heroine. Her older sister, Vanessa, is a college student who writes poetry and is active in the women's movement. Their mother, an artist of youthful promise, married at twenty and reared her children while relegating her artwork to the sidelines. Now she feels a deep sense of frustration and is a prime example of the unfulfilled woman so often delineated by feminists. In her early forties, Mother is experiencing a serious midlife crisis, constantly lamenting what she regards as the waste of her artistic talents. She nags her husband, claiming he does not understand her frustration. Though she is intelligent, energetic, and hardworking, she still cannot land a job. With no employment history to place on her resumé, she discovers that her talents, once so admired by others, are not immediately marketable. Nobody is willing to give an inexperienced housewife, regardless of her intelligence, an opportunity to prove herself. She becomes obsessed with the idea of earning thirty thousand dollars a year as a measure of self-worth.

Finally Dad, unable to endure the family turmoil any longer, leaves home and takes an apartment in New York City. Away from the distractions of suburban family life, he hopes to settle down and write his own long-planned novel. He also settles into an affair with a divorcée from his office. While Dad is away, mother receives the unsolicited attentions of the family lawyer, a gentle man whose son Mason likes Robin. Though the lawyer is married, his wife has been mentally ill for some time and has already left the family.

Dad's novel, rather sentimentally autobiographical, is considered good enough to be accepted for publication. His affair, which was a gesture of defiance he never took very seriously, comes to an end, and he returns home. Even Mother is by now beginning to come to terms with herself. The happy ending, in which the entire family is reconciled, is perhaps more wistfully reassuring than realistic for a family with so many frustrations.

It is the minor characters, even more than the central ones, who are used to promote the feminist message. Robin's maternal grandmother, the widow of a rich physician, is now living with her lover Joseph, who is a retired Russian professor and a skilled amateur musician. In one of the cozy family events that are not infrequent in these novels, Robin and Joseph shop for a splendid cello bow, which Grandmother is lavishly bestowing on him. Though Joseph is supported by the money that Grandfather left his widow, nobody in the family seems to mind. It is recognized that affluent women have as much right to provide for men they love as prosperous men have to keep unproductive wives or girlfriends who make them happy. Joseph is devoted to Grandmother, whom he has rescued from lonely widowhood and endowed with an active, eventful life.

Both Robin and her older sister, Vanessa, are feminists. Robin is seriously developing her talents as part of her self-realization. She gives music lessons during the summer and plays Bach and Beethoven with sensitivity and skill. Vanessa has strong anti-bourgeois attitudes, which she equates with feminism. She is especially distressed when her friend Wendy decides to marry a rich industrialist from the Midwest, a young man destined to join his father's prosperous but most unromantic dental supply business.

The women's rights movement believes in applying the same rules to both sexes. If men are allowed sexual experimentation, then women should receive the same privilege. This doctrine, which Klein accepts, leads logically to the sexual aggressiveness and openness found in her female characters. Robin exchanges kisses with Mason, the lawyer's son, and speculates about boys and sex. Her parents have been forthright with their children about their own sexual habits and are tolerant of the sexual explorations of the young. The "new morality," with its freer and more diverse sexual styles, is considered an option by everyone, young or old. But there are limits. During the course of the book, Mom and Dad try "open marriage" before eliminating it as a valid choice for themselves. Dad's friend from his New York office, Helen Becker, is thought to be promiscuous, and the family clearly rejects her as a role model; the predatory sexual style, when directed toward the fathers of families, is not one they are ready to accept. Vanessa brings her current lover home and is allowed to sleep with him there. Nobody sits in judgment on sexual experimentation by the unmarried, though the characters in *The Queen of the What Ifs* clearly articulate their conviction that sex without affection is meaningless.

Feminism extends the range of choice in many directions. One of Robin's friends gets pregnant and uses her new freedom to reject the ready option of abortion; she gets married instead. Going one step beyond feminism, Robin even at one point affirms that she sometimes actually desires to be a sex object and not just a person admired for her pleasing personality and diverse talents.

Not all problems are solved nor are all desired successes achieved. Vanessa gives a poetry reading in New York that is not too successful, though it is well attended by her supportive family. Mom learns how much her husband and children mean to her, even if her desire for a job and recognition for her art remain. She also learns to accept life in the suburbs, despite her earlier distaste for the values and style of suburbia. If Mother still thinks that her art would have flourished in the more stimulating environment of a big city, she at least acknowledges that family stability is more important to her than city adventure. Her picture of city life, as she knew it years before, is now somewhat idealized. She sees little beyond the cultural advantages of the city and is seemingly oblivious to the crime and bad management that are now the curse of life there. Again, the pro-New York sensibility of the book, which is that of the author as well as Mother, is not likely to endear it to regional teachers and librarians who feel young people are already too saturated with New York stories.

There are no truly unpleasant characters in this basically compassionate book, though Helen Becker and occasionally sister Vanessa come close. People are shown fumbling, making mistakes, doing the best they can, and usually progressing, however slowly, toward resolving their problems. Family ties, as always in Klein's books, are important. One does not lightly hurt others. Love and concern for the welfare of others, in fact, determine what is right and proper conduct. People have to find themselves, sometimes through painful experiences, but self-realization for women as well as for men is likely to lead to a new understanding of the value of family.

Love Is One of the Choices (1978) is another rather characteristic Klein narrative. Its length, 231 pages, is probably the chief reason it was published on the adult lists, though its subject matter is more appealing to young adults. The feminist dilemma is again especially well presented. Perhaps because it is so similar to other Klein books, *Publisher's Weekly* gave *Love Is One of the Choices* a rather harsh review, calling its events "artificial," its characters "so thin they cast no shadows," and its total effect little more than that of a series of dramatized polemical statements. The reviewer concluded, after examining precisely those elements calling forth the polemics—an affair between student and teacher, unmarried and married pregnancy, abortion, and feminist issues—that "the novel trails off instead of reaching a satisfying conclusion. The writing expresses no human feelings to speak of, least of all, any whiff of humor."[1]

This is too hasty a dismissal of Klein's narrative. First, Caroline, one of the two protagonists, is a new type of heroine for the author. She is a non-Jewish New Yorker, not particularly privileged, who lives with her mother, a pleasant woman who must work hard to make ends meet. Her father, who seems to be more affluent but is not very generous, makes documentary films in France and lives with a woman Caroline's mother primly refers to as his "common-law wife." Caroline sees little of him, though he does show up at her wedding near the end of the book.

Caroline's friend Maggie is Jewish. Since Maggie's mother has been dead for several years, she too is being reared by a single parent, her psychiatrist father. Though the friendship may seem a bit unlikely, it is not unrealistic, since close friends are frequently, perhaps usually, different in temperament. Maggie is much more aggressive than Caroline. As an outspoken feminist, she sometimes judges harshly the major decisions Caroline makes about her life. Fortunately for such an opinionated person, Maggie is a skilled debater. At one debate she is nevertheless demolished by Todd, who proceeds to ask her for a date. They start a long-lasting affair, though Maggie will not, for the present, let him speak of marriage.

Caroline, meanwhile, babysits with the young son of her high school science teacher, Justin, a man ten years older than herself. Justin's unstable wife, the daughter of a Nobel Prize–winning scientist, has long insisted on "an open marriage." By the time Caroline comes into the picture the wife has left home to live with her lover. With her long history of mental illness, nobody is very surprised when she subsequently commits suicide. Since Caroline is now graduating from high school and planning to study art at Parsons, Justin suggests she come live with him.

To Maggie's horror, Caroline not only moves in with Justin but decides to marry him as well. At the end of the book she is expecting a baby, despite Justin's own reservations about another child and Maggie's near rage at what she regards as Caroline's betrayal of feminist principles and her own potential. There is some hint that Caroline may be having a miscarriage (perhaps a rescue!), but the book ends on a note of ambiguity.

Maggie is, of course, a more complex and interesting character than Caroline. She is obviously fond of Todd Lamport, probably because he is the one man who can better her in debate, an area of expertise in which she takes pride, though she would certainly reject the suggestion that sensible women enjoy male domination. Todd himself is almost too ideal a character to be convincing. He is much more sympathetic and understanding of the quirks of a high-pressure young woman than a man of his youth might be expected to be. Neither of the leading males in the book is, in fact, particularly well realized. Justin seems little more than a bland, easygoing high school science teacher. The reader is asked to accept on faith that Justin and Todd are the interesting men their girlfriends find them to be, because they are not revealed by their actions or conversations to be exceptional.

Maggie, unlike Caroline, has an abortion when she becomes pregnant. Like other Klein characters, despite her liberal and feminist views, she feels surprisingly bad about it. It is clear that her pregnancy, even as she rejects it, has been a statement. Though her father, alert to his responsibilities as a single parent, had earlier sent her to a gynecologist to be fitted with a diaphragm, she either did not use it properly or an accident occurred. There is some inevitable speculation about subconscious intentions by the principal characters themselves; Maggie is, after all, like Klein the daughter of a Freudian psychiatrist. Motivations, whether conscious or otherwise, are never made fully clear, just as in real life they are rarely totally evident.

Though Caroline has talent and unusual beauty, she never gets to experiment with life or to become acquainted with a variety of men. She knows only Justin, who seems to please her. Perhaps she will be happier in life than Maggie. Again the reader cannot be sure whether Caroline is fortunate in finding the man she loves so soon, before she has had other experiences, or if she will live to regret her impulsive, youthful choice. There is, of course, no suggestion that happiness and self-realization are the same. The typical Klein reader is almost certain to find Caroline unappealing, the very model of much that the liberated woman dislikes. Yet the author obviously intends her to be taken seriously. Caroline's choices have an ambiguity that is always found in life, less frequently in fiction. Maggie, on the other hand, may appear to know what she wants out of life, but she is not very happy. She is becoming world-weary at an early age. The conclusion of the book is, again, indecisive. Klein, as always, is aware that feminism not only brings liberation to women who accept it, but also perplexities and burdens as well.

There is, however, the customary string of marriages or unions to bring this narrative, again like that Renaissance comedy, to its end. Maggie's father, to everyone's surprise, marries his long-standing girlfriend, and Caroline's previously inhibited mother, even more surprisingly, lets her boyfriend move into her apartment.

Klein's usual shopping list of violated taboos (early marriage, teacher-student sex, and abortion) is evident, though it is not precisely clear just whose taboos they are. Young marriage is one of Klein's own; she does not normally advocate it, but does permit it in this narrative. Love is, after all, one of the choices; not everyone must or can accept the liberated woman's credo. In most

American social groups there would still be considerable concern over a high school teacher who seduces one of his students, or allows himself to be seduced by her, especially if she is his son's babysitter. His subsequent marriage to her would not wipe out all objection. Such an event might even become a feminist issue. Abortion is always a ready option in a Klein novel and Caroline is, in this context, more unconventional for her refusal to allow herself to be talked into one. She is, after all, happily married and sees no reason not to welcome a child. While Maggie does have an abortion, she does not respond to the event with the composure called for by her feminist stance.

While Klein has again in the character of Maggie presented a strong object lesson of feminism at work, in this book she has also revealed herself once more to be the defender of home and hearth as much as the soul sister of Gloria Steinem and Bella Abzug.

6. Family Styles: "Different Ways of Loving"

Perhaps nothing in recent years has changed more in books for young people than the presentation of family life. The earlier ideal was the two-parent home, with a house of lively children, plus a dog and cat. Mother, often matronly in appearance, welcomed children home from school with a plate of cookies, while father returned from his office in the evening. This idealized family, which dominated genteel juvenile fiction, may never have reflected very accurately the reality of home life in the Western world. Today it is impossible even to maintain the fiction. In a large number of families both parents work, either because two paychecks are necessary or because both have careers they choose not to abandon. Vast numbers of children are also being reared by single parents, and sometimes the single parent is Father. Families are now generally smaller than before. *Cheaper by the Dozen*-style coziness would be considered tasteless in a contemporary young adult novel, just as it has come to be considered irresponsible in real life.

In the recent juvenile fiction, which is sometimes referred to as "the new realism," parents are not only allowed to have faults, but they may also have sex lives, and not necessarily with a marital partner. In fact, the partner may not even be of the opposite sex. Gay people may be shown working hard at parenting

74

just the same as anyone else. They may even be presented as good role models for their children. In still other books, Mother may never have been married at all, despite the fact that she is a successful professional of the middle class rather than an impoverished ghetto woman. Sex roles are no longer clearly differentiated; while Mother more often than not holds a job, sometimes Father is a househusband, commendably caring for the children. Juvenile novels in which Father is the chief nurturer of children first gained recognition in Scandinavia and are no longer the novelties they once were in the United States.

Several of Norma Klein's most interesting books have presented family styles that would have been designated unorthodox only a few years ago. *Mom, the Wolf Man and Me* (1972) was the first and is still the most discussed. It remains one of the best of the new-style family stories by any author. To date, it is the only Klein book that has been followed by a film version. Though technically a middle-grade book, rather than a young adult novel, it is safe to say that it has been read by every serious Klein fan. A genuine work of literature, it transcends publisher's usual categories as a true "crossover."

Probably because its heroine was eleven and the book was designed chiefly for readers who were eight to twelve years old, the book caused a furor on publication. Not only had the young heroine's mother never been married, but she admitted to her daughter that she had had sex with her current boyfriend, after he showed up at breakfast one morning in pajamas. The controversy was probably intensified by the undeniable literary quality of the narrative. Not only was it skillfully constructed, but there were believable, likable characters and a plot that, even if somewhat static, sustained interest. The book had to be taken seriously, like it or not. First discussions concentrated on the middle-class unmarried mother, the book's acknowledgement, though not with details, of her active sex life, and her daughter's joyful acceptance of the one-parent family status. As her first published book, *Mom, the Wolf Man and Me* established Klein's early reputation as a gifted writer of family stories with unconventional situations. Several ingredients assured the success of the book. Not only was there a loving, if slightly odd family, which included eccentric grandparents, but there was an irresistibly attractive dog named Norma. Added to this was the appealing child heroine, who gained a measure of maturity and understanding from her experiences. There was even a happy ending. Nevertheless, the narrative still managed to avoid sentimentality.

The plot line of *Mom, the Wolf Man and Me* is simple. The parents of Brett Levin, the eleven-year-old heroine and first-person narrator, have never been married. Brett has little curiosity about her natural father, whom she has not met. Content with her mother's sole attentions in ways that even an only child usually cannot know, Brett sees no need for a father. Children in two-parent families, she observes, have to eat three meals a day, on time, keep a strict bedtime routine, and must wear skirts instead of jeans. Brett loves the life-style she shares with Deborah, her mother, and the freedoms and privileges denied children in more regular family situations. For example, she and Mom have flexible eating schedules, dress as they please, and attend protest marches in Washington. They are also best friends, companions who are always frank with one another. Deborah is totally unlike the media stereotype of a single mother; she is no welfare woman striving to feed her child and keep her out of mischief. Instead, she is a talented professional photographer. Deborah is also fortunate in having parents who accept and support her, even though they sometimes regard her choices as strange. Her father, a psychoanalyst with a rich imagination, is always sharing childhood fantasies with his granddaughter. At one point the two of them pretend he is keeping a pet alligator in the bathtub.

Brett has some interesting friends who serve as foils for her and her mother and amusingly flesh out the social setting in which the action unfolds. Evelyn, about Brett's age, is the child of divorced parents. Unlike Brett, she constantly longs for a father and feels her life will not be complete until her mother finds an appropriate one for her. She even pretends the Tin Man in *The Wizard of Oz* is her dad. Evelyn's beautiful mother is indeed always going out on dates, an earnest activity her daughter is certain is a calculated campaign to find the desired father. Yet mother, despite all her effort, has so little luck that at one point she attempts suicide by taking an overdose of sleeping pills. Events are seen opaquely, from the child's point of view. Fortunately Evelyn's mother is able to pull herself together and continue her personal quest.

Andrew is the playmate Brett loves best. Unlike Brett and Evelyn, he has a regular family, with a father who is a rabbi. His dad, who has a handsome beard and appears very elegant to the children, always talks in a deep voice, like a character in a play. Brett cannot overcome the feeling that he is not quite real. When he speaks, it is as though he has thought out the whole sentence ahead of time, complete with all the periods and commas. Andrew and his family keep a strict Sabbath; while Brett's mother and grandparents are Jewish, they do no more than make jokes about Sabbath observance. Although Andrew's father is not himself radical and is skeptical of demonstrations, he does allow his son to accompany Brett and her mother on a protest march to Washington.

Problems, however, soon arise to mar the tranquillity of Brett's happy two-person family. She attends an animal fashion show where she meets a strangely wonderful and funny-looking man with red hair, pock-marked skin, and a splendid Irish wolfhound named Norma. She calls him "The Wolf Man" and introduces him to her mother, thinking Mom will also enjoy knowing Norma. The Wolf Man, it turns out, comes from Montana, teaches special children who are slow learners, and makes marvelous homemade bread. Mother is as intrigued by the Wolf Man as Brett is by his dog. To Brett's utter amazement and total displeasure, Deborah begins to consider marriage. Both daughter and dog are at first extremely jealous. Brett does not wish to share her mother even with anyone as special as the Wolf Man, and Norma is equally reluctant to relinquish the exclusive attentions of her best friend, companion, and master. Brett mulls over her problem:

> I really don't think Mom should get married. I don't think she would like it, because she isn't used to it. If you're married, you have to live a certain way. You have to do things at certain

times. Also I guess I'm afraid Mom would be different if she
was married. She would be more like Andrew's mother, and
probably wouldn't take me places. She and The Wolf Man would
do things together, and I would have to stay at home with some
babysitter like Mrs. Wizen, which I would hate. Besides, they
don't allow dogs in our building, so The Wolf Man would have
to keep a special apartment just for Norma, and that would be
expensive. There are lots of reasons against it and not that
many for. But I think Mom knows that. She wouldn't just go
and do it. She's not like that.

Brett's mother, too, has her reservations about marriage, even
after she decides to go through with it. She acknowledges that
her friends will think she is renouncing her principles in order
to join bourgeois society. Experiencing wedding jitters the day
before the ceremony, she laments: "Oh, it's awful . . . giving in
to convention like this. Why did I let the two of you [Brett and
the Wolf Man] convince me to go ahead with it?" Brett rightly
feels this a strange accusation, since she had originally struggled
against the marriage. The festivities take place at the home of a
friend who is an animal trainer; animals are all around, including,
of course, Norma, who will continue to be an important member
of the new family. A Unitarian minister—reliable standby for
nonobservant Jews—is brought in to conduct the marriage ceremony, since he can be trusted not to intrude too much religiosity.
At the end, Brett is reconciled to her new family and is looking
forward to moving to Arizona where the Wolf Man has a new job.

It was noted by the first reviewers that though Klein's book
conveys the message that an unmarried mother may head a happy
home and create a healthy environment for successfully rearing
a child, this book, despite its daring message, concludes with the
conventional Hollywood happy ending. The reader, even when
ready to accept the original family style of Brett and her mother,
is nevertheless conditioned to expect a wedding at the end and is
not disappointed.[1]

Mom, the Wolf Man and Me, placed in any literary category,
should be judged a fine achievement, particularly for a first published novel. Its quality did not pass unnoticed upon publication,

but, as is too often the case, reviewers were more inclined to evaluate the book as bibliotherapy than as literature. The favorable review in *School Library Journal* was not atypical: "Norma Klein has a fund of right ideas of life and is giving them to just the right age group. . . . Rich characters and dynamic interactions, much humor and warmth are the book's justification. Best of all, the author makes readers aware that their lives will be shaped by the values they have. And it's all done without preaching!"[2]

Already in this her first book the strengths of the characteristic Klein story may be observed: the satirical humor, the warmth of the family setting, the introduction of an unusual, slightly shocking lifestyle, the well-developed characters, and the lively, convincing dialogue. The somewhat pat resolution and ending may well be a concession to the genre, whose conventions Klein continues sometimes to honor and sometimes to defy.

Taking Sides (1974) is another strong early book, equally notable for its sustained narrative, its fine character development, and its warm depiction of another unusual family situation. Also a middle book, it has, like *Mom, the Wolf Man and Me* enjoyed a strong older readership as well. It was Klein's earliest contribution to the subgenre of family story in which the father is the prime nurturer of the children. Nell, the first-person narrator, and her little brother, Hugo, live with their father in the city. On weekends they visit their mother, who lives outside New York with her friend Greta. Mom and Dad, Nell informs the reader, have been married and separated twice. Though there is some bitterness that is never fully explained, they certainly try to act for the best interests of their children. The strong implication is that Mother's likely lesbian tendencies have made a sustained marriage difficult, although the reader is wisely left to reach his or her own conclusions. Both parents, while responsibly rearing Nell and Hugo, are trying to reconstruct lives of their own. Dad has a girlfriend, the wealthy and stylish Arden, who sometimes stays overnight. At one point she accompanies him and the children on vacation to Jamaica. All the characters, with the possible exception of Arden, are decent if imperfect people trying to do their best. Their problems and ways of coping with a broken family are believable.

Nell herself is especially well drawn. The central conflict is her preference for her father, whom she adores, over her mother, whom she likes and respects. The family has made the calm, rational decision that Dad is better able to care for the children in his apartment than Mother in the Victorian house she shares with Greta. Mom is away all day at her office job, and Greta feels unequipped psychologically to take care of children, although she later becomes very attached to Hugo. Since Dad is a free-lance writer of science books, he works at home and has a more flexible schedule for child care. With the weekend visits, however, the children are in contact with the other household. Since Mom, employed as a computer programmer, earns more than Dad, she shoulders a greater financial responsibility for the children.

Nell enjoys Dad's household. She likes being the central female in his life and playing mother, in a sense, to Hugo, even though she really wishes Hugo would go to live with Mom, who is his favorite parent. Dad always provides the delicacies loved by children, such as tuna fish and hamburgers. He buys Nell lovely clothes and treats her as a friend as well as a daughter. While she does not much approve of Arden, Nell does not feel seriously threatened by the competition for his attentions. She is, however, relieved when Arden throws a tantrum and disappears from his life.

As in most of Klein's books, there are some especially interesting minor characters. Nell enjoys her friends in the city. Arlo, her boyfriend, is also being reared by his father, because his mother is an invalid. Again, Klein juxtaposes the family situation of her heroine with other similar or contrasting family arrangements. Another friend Nell's age is the elegant Heather, who comes from a family of fashion models. Since Heather has always been beautiful, she takes her looks for granted. She has started refusing to model; though she cannot yet articulate her reasons, she is certainly making her own feminist statement by rejecting the family trade, so obviously based on exploitation of the physical attributes of women. There is realistic and amusing girltalk between her and Nell. They discuss how hard it is for a young woman to know what the acceptable rules of conduct are today. Ann Landers, they conclude, may ultimately be the only guide.

Greta, Mom's house companion, is also a well-realized character, though Klein wisely does not overexplain her. A vegetarian who smokes constantly, she obviously has her eccentricities and compulsions. Though she and Mom share a bedroom, they appear to have separate beds, and they always conduct themselves with discretion. In Greta's rambling and comfortable New Jersey house, Mom is ensconced like an old-fashioned china doll. In the evenings Greta plays the flute for her. Nell's grandmother, who has her own problems with alcohol, disapproves of Greta, ostensibly because she says it is not right for a person to live on inherited money and not work, as does Greta. It is, however, probable that Grandma is unable to come to terms with the nature of Greta's relationship with her daughter.

Nell's life, however, is not without conflict. Dad has a heart attack, bringing an end to her lovely year in his apartment. Other arrangements must be made for the children, at least temporarily. Nell has often thought that the worst possible thing she could ever imagine would be to lose her father. Yet she learns how to cope with his potentially fatal illness, contending successfully even with this crisis in the pivotal year of her life.

Taking Sides is a strong work, which deserves to be judged on its literary strengths. Many reviewers, however, had already taken their stand on Norma Klein and were responding as much to her personality and philosophy as to her skills in her craft.

Alice Bach, who distinctly disliked the book, based her objections as much on ethical as on literary grounds in her *New York Times Book Review* analysis: "Norma Klein has packaged a piece of meretricious reassurance, the lying about life that has signaled the sloppiest of children's fiction since Nancy Drew solved every case just in the nick of time. Admitting to children the uncertainty of life is far more honest than this book, which pretends at reality through the mention of 10-speed bikes, vegetarians and an Afro doll named Calef. The pain of sickness, the tensions of separation, the fear of death are as deeply felt here as the steamroller that momentarily flattens a cartoon character."[3]

With her clever use of language, her ability to turn a memorable phrase, Bach was especially devastating in her conclusion: "Since Norma Klein has chosen to act as faithful scribe to trendy teen-age dialogue and scattered teen-age thoughts, she has avoided the writer's essential task—to reflect upon and shape the material of the novel with a special perspective, a vision unique to each writer's imagination. By blunting the writer's sharpest tool, the imaginative use of language, she has denied the reader a sense of place or orientation in the world that the novel purports to create."[4]

Most other critics were not so harsh as Bach in their judgments, concluding that Klein had handled the parents well, not in an idealized fashion but with sympathy and understanding, making them believably real individuals with genuine strengths and flaws. Klein's treatment of sexuality was also generally commended, especially in the understatement of the probable lesbian relationship.

Breaking Up, published six years later, in 1980, was in part inspired by the discussion and speculation stirred by the female parent in *Taking Sides.* It should be acknowledged that Klein has always denied creating the Mom-Greta relationship as a gay liberation statement, insisting that she did not know for sure herself if their relationship was sexual and had given it little thought until discussion ensued. Now she admits that indeed the relationship must have been lesbian and further contends that she should have made its nature clearer in the narrative. In *Breaking Up* there is no such ambiguity.

Though lesbian parenthood has been the most frequently discussed feature of *Breaking Up,* it is not the book's central idea. *Breaking Up* is another story of teenage love and exploration; unfortunately, it is not one of Klein's best. Ali and her brother Martin leave their mother in New York to visit their father in California. He and his second wife decide that the children should remain with them on the West Coast, especially when they learn of Mother's sexual orientation. Mother honestly acknowledges her sexual preference and feels no apologies are needed. She is also ready, if necessary, to fight for her rights to her children. She even comes to California to protect her interests, though she has injured her leg in an automobile accident and is in discomfort throughout her trip. There is, however, no nasty scene; these are civilized people, who are able to work out a compromise. Ali and her friends have already speculated in school about Eleanor Roosevelt's sexual inclinations. The fact that the former First Lady is thought by some biographers to have had a physical attachment to another woman makes them all feel better about gay people.

California suits Martin fine, because his girlfriend, with whom he is having a heated relationship, lives there. Though Ali too has a boyfriend in California, she feels she cannot abandon her mother and consequently chooses to return to New York. After resettling in her mother's new apartment, she becomes comfortable enough with homosexual choices to be able to show her boyfriend, when he finally visits her in New York, the bedroom that Mother and the female lover share.

Breaking Up is a much less interesting book than *Taking Sides,* perhaps in part because the conflict it sets in motion is not sustained. The reader cannot shake off the impression that the author was less concerned with telling a story about a young woman's family conflicts than with making a statement about sexual liberation in general. The teenage characters spend an inordinate amount of time in bed with one another, rather meaninglessly exploring their awakened sexuality. The genuine dynamics of the lesbian relationship, unfortunately, are ignored. Klein misses a fine opportunity to examine the perplexities of a woman who has lived for many years as a heterosexual before finding the courage to acknowledge her true sexual nature with her female lover. The relationship between the father and his second wife, who reads books on being a good stepmother and makes real effort but somehow never seems able to bring it off, could also have been more amusingly developed. Klein has created several potentially interesting characters, but has made little of them.

Another opportunity is lost through a failure to develop meaningfully the conflicts between East and West Coasts and explore the differences in manners and mores. There is some mention, indeed, of the dangers of living in New York City. Ali comments that in their former apartment someone always seemed to be getting mugged; now that they have moved across the street to the brownstone residence of Mother's lover, she feels much safer. Dad and his friends in California think of New York as a city of "grime and crime," of sexual perversion. Nevertheless, regional attitudes and prejudices remain largely uninvestigated.

Though Dad and his wife fear that Mother's sexual preferences will have an adverse effect on Ali, there seems to be no effect at all. After many preliminaries, Ali agrees to a physical relationship with her boyfriend. Having established beyond question her own heterosexual preferences, she then separates from him for a year, while she returns to New York to be with her mother. She muses: "It'll be hard being apart all year. I almost wish I had stayed out in Berkeley. But then Mom might have thought I didn't approve of her and Peggy and I wouldn't want her to feel that way. There are just different ways of loving people, that's all; there's no one right way. I guess you have to sort of figure it out as you go along."

The moral of the book seems clearly to be that "we should respect individual differences because that is what makes life interesting." At the end, Ali and her mother acknowledge that the year has brought a coming-of-age enlightenment, with Ali gaining insight into the lives of both parents as well as an understanding of her own feelings.

Reviewers quickly pointed out that Klein had been so intent on making her sexual liberation statement that she had marred her narrative with a fallacious and unnecessary contrast. In order to show that there are different styles of successful loving and that an individual's choice must be his or her own, Klein presented the lesbian mother and her lover in an extremely favorable light, as well-adjusted, generous, and happy individuals. By way of contrast, Ali's father and his wife, an insecure therapist, seem confused, uncertain, and bumbling.[5] This is valid criticism; *Breaking Up* is one of Klein's few forgettable books.

Family Secrets (1985) is another weak book that attempts to explore problems besetting teenagers in disintegrating families. The leading characters, Leslie and Peter, are finishing high school and planning for college, at Harvard and the University of Chicago, respectively. Leslie is also busy rehearsing for the senior play, *The Barretts of Wimpole Street,* in which she is to have great success in the role of Elizabeth Barrett Browning's sister. This play about attachment of daughters to fathers serves as a thematic backdrop to the story of family crisis. Though Peter feels he is too fat and a bit of a misfit, he is able to catch Leslie's attention, and they begin an affair. To their horror they discover that Leslie's glamorous mother and Peter's equally dashing father, an actor in television commercials, are leaving their current spouses to marry each other.

Leslie and Peter, who end up living in the same apartment with the newly constituted couple, feel awkward and somewhat incestuous. Although they believe they love each other, their relationship does not progress well. Peter's vain and insecure father, who must attract the attention of every woman he encounters, even tries to flirt with Leslie. Though he is unsuccessful in his efforts to entice her, Peter's father is soon having affairs with other women, as has always been his habit. His new marriage breaks up before it has hardly begun.

Life for Leslie and Peter is not pleasant in their new home. Peter must cope with his father's constant ridicule about his weight, and Leslie has never been very comfortable with her mother. Even before the new marriage collapses, Leslie has decided that she will return to her father, taking Peter with her. As the two young people start a cross-country trip together, there appears some chance that their relationship will mature, despite the poor role models their parents have given them. Peter's father, who has always been an empty person, will continue to be surrounded by attractive women, even though he will never make deep commitments to any of them. Leslie's mother is left alone, devastated, though probably no wiser for her matrimonial misadventure.

Family Secrets, despite its potentially interesting family situation, remains one of Klein's thinner books. The narrative holds the reader's attention but without being provocative, and the characters are sympathetic without being memorable. Klein does, to her credit, identify some of the problems that may be faced by sensitive young people drawn into the new, temporary families that may be briefly constructed, in this era of quick marriage and no-fault divorce.

The Sunshine books, of which Klein wrote three, are novelizations of television scenarios. Though novelizations are frequently pulled together in haste to cash in on the popularity of narratives first appearing in other media, Klein obviously lavished considerable attention on these books. They are well done. She was able to expand the material originated by others in order to express several themes that are important to her. Another unorthodox family situation is presented in the Sunshine series, and, despite the strangeness of the home setting, a child is shown being reared successfully.

Sunshine (1975), the first and most interesting volume of the little trilogy, was based on a rather sentimental though generally effective television script written by Carol Sobieski. The plot was suggested by a real occurrence, the death of Jacquelyn M. Helton at the age of nineteen. In addition to an infant daughter, Helton left behind some moving journals intended to be read in later years by her child. In the novelization, Kate, the fictional portrait of Jacquelyn, is a young hippie type who, even though she is pregnant, deserts a husband she cannot love and parents she has always resented. She meets, moves in with, and finally marries Sam, a pop musician. By the time, however, that the couple is wed, Kate is already in a hospital bed dying of bone cancer. Sam is kind and loving, even though, understandably in view of his own youth, he has difficulty coming to terms with his wife's illness. While she is dying, he has an affair with a neighbor as a form of escape. Yet he loves Kate very much and has no intention of abandoning her or her child. The development of Kate's cancer, which starts with a small spot on her leg and progresses to debilitating proportions, is realistically detailed. She refuses medication when she discovers its unpleasant side effects and that it will only prolong and not save her life. Fortunately she has an understanding doctor, who grants her requests even though her husband is troubled when she rejects treatment.

Kate's child is charmingly described, and the joy of youthful motherhood is convincingly conveyed. Klein is frequently at her best when introducing infants into her narratives, and her powers of characterization do not fail her here. Though the child is not his own flesh and blood, Sam accepts it as if it were and plans to rear the little girl after his wife is gone. Kate writes poems, chiefly inspired by her daughter. They are not especially good poems, but they are sensitive and interestingly countercultural, convincing for the time and place in which they were written. Despite Kate's illness and Sam's grief, there are moments of family happiness. A pastoral picnic is especially well described. It is clear that in later years Sam's memory of this period will be bathed in a mellow afterglow.

Following the television script, the bulk of the action of *Sunshine* takes place in Vancouver, a new locale for Klein. Kate and Sam are expatriate Americans living in Canada. Though there is no attempt at verisimilitude of location, this is no flaw in the story; attention is focused on events of personal life that would have unfolded in the same way almost anywhere.

The pace of the book is rather slow. As usual, Klein does not rely on suspense to generate the interest of her story; the interactions of personalities hold the reader's attention. Indeed, the characters are much better realized than those generally found in novelizations from other media. Kate and Sam speak realistically and have relationships, emotions, and even inconsistencies of personality that are believable.

Not all the action, however, is well motivated or entirely believable. It is never really clear why the pregnant Kate leaves her first husband, the father of her child. When he finally makes an appearance in the book, it is apparent that he is not an unkind man. Though he cares for his child, he does not choose to assert his parental rights to the detriment of others. The reader begins to suspect that it was his position as a member of conventional society, rather than the counterculture, that made him unacceptable to Kate. She merely explains that she found him insensitive.

The message Kate wants to leave her daughter, through her journals and the memories her family and friends retain, is not surprising, considering her youth and Bohemian lifestyle. It is, however, a questionable guide for life: do what you want; that is the way to live.

Klein was obviously alert to the dangers of ready-made sentimentality in the *Sunshine* situation: the death of a teenage mother and the rearing of an orphaned child by a young pop musician stepfather. Going to some pains to avoid making her story a trite tearjerker, Klein resorted to the old author's trick of preparing an audience in advance to accept some otherwise embarrassing or hackneyed sequence of events. As if to affirm her determination to avoid the staged handkerchief-wringing scene, Klein has Kate contrast her own uncomfortable death with the glamorous death, in the Camille tradition, of the heroine of Erich Segal's *Love Story:*

> I keep thinking of that movie, *Love Story,* which we saw awhile back. It makes me angry even thinking of it. Her husband was so perfect, so kind, and she always was so lovely—she never even went for medication! Christ! That's so unrealistic! Movies like that should be banned, I think. They make the whole thing so unreal, as though you could die without pain or ugliness. I feel I'm learning something from all this, but at times I'm not sure I want to. I'm not sure I want to see things in Sam, see his weaknesses. How come *her* hair didn't fall out? Why didn't she throw up every day? How come they never argued about anything because they were both scared and angry at the unfairness of it all! Oh, calm down, Kate. Don't go off ranting. What purpose does that serve? Just get it off my chest, I guess.

Klein has admitted to finding ideas for her fiction by watching television, listening to her children talk, and observing the lives of her friends. With the successful Sunshine books, she demonstrated her considerable skill in adapting stories from another medium, in many ways improving on the original in the process. The Sunshine television programs obviously gave her stronger material to work with than the thin film script of *Postcards,* her other fictionalization. She was genuinely moved by the plight of a dying teenage mother and the problems of the surviving husband trying conscientiously to provide for the child who was not his kin but rather his responsibility and the memento of a bittersweet marriage.

Though Klein rarely writes sequels, the two subsequent Sunshine books are exceptions. She decided to carry the experiences of Sam and Jill through two additional books. *The Sunshine Years* (1975) was the first. It was also based on a television program, with several incidents drawn from episodes by other writers.

The Sunshine Years takes the characters ahead several years in time. Jill is six years old and her stepfather, still earning a living as a country-rock singer, is working hard to give her a happy childhood; his top priority has become her welfare. At her request, he even invites her natural father for a visit. Now married to a career woman who does not want children, Jill's real father does not ask for custody. Yet he indicates his desire to maintain contact and promises to write Jill from France, where he is employed. He buys her a fine dollhouse, his notion of a proper gift for a little girl, though Jill actually prefers the cruder, sometimes-homemade toys Sam provides.

Meanwhile Sam decides he owes it to the child to get married. Bowing to convention, he decides Jill will benefit from a more settled home life. The nice woman next door, Nora, who serves as a surrogate mother for Jill and with whom Sam had that brief, consoling affair while his wife was on her deathbed, is the likely choice. Although she is fond of him and sleeps with him with some regularity, Nora turns down Sam's proposal. She has already been unhappily married, at an earlier period in her life, and has concluded that "marriage messes up your head." Sam next meets a glamorous singer with whom he has a halfhearted affair, but she too refuses marriage, announcing that not only does she prefer a career to family life but she has just accepted a job performing on a cruise ship.

Sam's mother in Texas volunteers to take Jill. While she is well-meaning, she has difficulty relating to young children and is uncomfortable with the lifestyle to which Sam and Jill have become accustomed. The reader is glad that Sam decides he will not allow her to adopt Jill.

Sam's child-rearing methods, though unorthodox, are shown to be sound. He is open with Jill and does not hide from her that he is sleeping with his girlfriends. Sam and Jill have frank conversations about sex, even though her interests in the subject seem a bit premature. A complaint, however, is lodged with the Canadian Child Welfare Department, and an agent comes to investigate. Sam and his friends stage a potentially amusing scene, complete with home-style beef roast, trying to convince the agent of their domesticity, believing she will equate that with his fitness to rear the child. The scene in which Sam and his friends simulate a traditional home-and-hearth seems chiefly designed for visual impact on television, and it is not brought off successfully in the novel. The reader is no more taken in by it than is the Canadian social worker. But she turns out to be both more sophisticated and more sympathetic than everyone expects. Despite his bachelor lifestyle and method of earning his living, Sam, the social worker concludes, is an acceptable parent.

Jill is a happy little girl, enjoying a life of more freedom and diversity than a child growing up in a conventional family would be allowed. She is the pet not only of Sam but of his musician friends and girlfriends. Refried beans for breakfast are fine with her, and there is always Nora next door, both Sam's favorite girlfriend and Jill's best female role model.

Sunshine Christmas (1977) is somewhat less successful than the two preceding books, although it manages a few convincing scenes. Sam returns with Jill to his hometown in Texas for the holiday. Even though he must brace himself for the ordeal of confronting his small-town parents for an extended time, he decides a traditional family Christmas is important for Jill. By now Nora has overcome her resistance to marriage, acquired a rich husband, and is not available for the kind of maternal care she was once able to provide Jill. Sam comes into immediate conflict with the attitudes of the Texas town he had earlier escaped. His father, who is a newspaperman, represents, not surprisingly, the very middle-class values that the musician son has repudiated.

Though Sam makes an effort to adjust and even contemplates marrying one of the local women, whom he remembers affectionately from high school, both he and Jill eventually conclude it will not work and that they must leave.

The characterization of Jill is not so successful here as it was in the previous books. Though she is still described as "a ray of sunshine," she now strikes the reader as a bit of a brat. For example, at Nora's wedding she has a vicious fight with one of Nora's new stepsons. Just as readily, she falls for the bribes her grandparents give to win her favor, and they almost succeed in weaning her away from Sam.

The characters who populate Sam's Texas hometown are tiresome stereotypes. Their conversations amount to little more than media small-town clichés. Sam's old high school flame, Cody, now a widow running a saloon-restaurant, is one of the least believable characters in the entire Klein canon. She seems to be an update of Kitty, right out of the old television Western "Gunsmoke." Cody is so obliging as mistress and prospective wife to Sam that it seems out of character when she ultimately rejects his plea that she return to Vancouver with him. She explains, not too persuasively, that she has made her peace with her hometown and now does not want to leave it.

Central to *Sunshine Christmas* is the conflict between the happy if irregular family style of Sam and Jill and the traditional home life of Sam's parents. Father and son are incapable of an extended civil conversation, so great is their antagonism and the discrepancy between their values. Sam despises small-town life, while his parents believe the small town, with its churches and schools, is the only proper place to rear a child. When Sam's patience is exhausted, he gets on his motorbike, preparing to return to Vancouver. Jill, who at first seems won over by her foster grandparents, finds she cannot bear to see him leave; she runs after him down the road, waving her duffel bag and calling, "Wait for me, Daddy!" Father and daughter, who form a genuine family, will not be separated.

The Swap, a 1983 novel, was published on the adult lists, largely because of its 314 pages. It is, however, of principal interest to younger people. It is one of the most curious and intriguing of all Klein's books, chiefly because it introduces the strangest of her family situations. The chief characters are not the usual New Yorkers readers have come to expect, and they do not come from the upper middle class. Nor are they people of culture. Auburn, the town in which the action largely takes place, is admittedly patterned after the tiny college town in upstate New York where Norma Klein's husband grew up; the small college mentioned in the narrative would seem to be a fictionalized Wells, the school where his parents taught.

The main characters in *The Swap,* Maddy and Jed, do not attend college but go to Auburn as a young married couple holding low-paying jobs. Their aspirations, at least initially, do not lead them beyond the unskilled labor pool of a college campus or staff work in a beauty salon. By the end of the book their horizons have expanded, though they have, in rejecting the responsibilities of marriage and parenthood, badly failed their first tests of adulthood. What they have done, in fact, is traded their baby for a new car. (While this is their major swap, they have also indulged in a bit of husband-and-wife swapping along the way.) After completing their transaction, they have blithely gone their separate ways, the young man uncertain of the next chapter in his life and the young woman assured of a promising job on the West Coast. Picking up the pieces of her life, Maddy, at least, seems on her way to modest personal and occupational success.

Some readers, not surprisingly, have found *The Swap* repugnant. Admittedly the plot is improbable, though most readers become absorbed in the provocative situations and characters. There is an especially striking counterpoint established between the two young female characters, Maddy, the modest, traditional, lower middle-class wife, and Capri, the overprivileged, liberated, and sexually free college student.

At the beginning of the narrative, Maddy is ousted from her Roman Catholic working-class home when she becomes pregnant by her high school boyfriend, Jed. Though Maddy loves him, Jed himself is merely on the rebound from another girl, whose prosperous family has rejected him as a suitor. Initially professing some pale intentions of fulfilling his personal responsibilities, he takes Maddy home, where he lives with his dad. Though his father, a kindly, tolerant man, asks no questions, Jed decides to marry Maddy properly before the baby comes. This is largely thanks to the urging of his best friends, another teenage couple already married. Jed takes a job on the maintenance staff of the small private college and moves with his new family into employee housing.

He has not been on campus long before he meets Capri, a beautiful, spoiled coed from the city, described as the prototypical "Jewish-American Princess." Her parents, a rich physician and his fashionable wife, have banished her from Harvard because of her many self-indulgences, and she is bored on a small, dull campus. Jed begins a long affair with her that almost gets him fired when her father learns of it and protests in fury to college officials. Though Jed asks Capri to marry him, not surprisingly, she declines. Not only is he already married, but she has often proclaimed her intention of remaining unmarried until the age of thirty. Apart from career plans, she has more glamorous matrimonial ambitions than he could ever fulfill. He is slowly forced to realize that she has been using him to get through a tiresome school year until she can convince her parents to send her back to Harvard, where she knows her prospects are better.

Maddy accepts sex to please Jed, without deriving much enjoyment from it. Capri, on the other hand, loves having sex and is insatiable. Here the bright, liberated woman easily wins in competition with the sweet, mousy, overworked one, especially with social-climbing Jed. While Klein claims she had much sympathy for Jed while she was composing the book, viewing him as a young man almost unwittingly entrapped with family responsibility, she provided him with so little strength of character that he must still be identified as one of the few truly unappealing persons in her fiction. He is totally self-centered, has no paternal instincts, and appears incapable of any empathy with Maddy and her problems.

When the baby is born, both Maddy and Jed are disappointed that it is a girl. Furthermore, the child has crossed eyes and in their judgment is quite ugly. Because they can think of no better name, they call her Minnie. Seeing Jed's lack of affection for the baby and his habit of staying away from home until all hours, Maddy concludes that the child's crying is driving him from their meager apartment. She believes that her marriage will improve if she can dispose of the child. First she offers it to a neighbor, who politely turns her down. Then she gets the idea of offering the infant to Mr. Edelman, a used-car salesman for whom Jed has worked. Though Mr. Edelman might appear an unlikely savior, Maddy's intuition, for once, turns out to be valid. He is a widower who has recently lost both his son and grandchild in an automobile accident. He enthusiastically accepts Maddy's offer; feeling rejuvenated by the care of a small child, he sells his used-car lot in order to move to Florida where he believes he can give Minnie a better life. Though he expects to devote himself to the child's welfare, he has another dream to realize as well. He has long wanted to be a teacher rather than a businessman, and now he believes that circumstances will finally permit him to follow his long-delayed vocation.

There are really two separate plots in the novel, which converge with the gift of the baby. What starts as a gift becomes "the swap" when Mr. Edelman in gratitude gives Jed a fine red Z-28 Camaro. Jed, who feels he is getting by far the better deal, considers Edelman insane to trade such a fine machine for a cross-eyed baby. Mr. Edelman's own story is the other focus of the book. Respected as a member of what is widely regarded as a rare breed, honest used-car dealers, Edelman is successful in business but is a lonely man. In keeping with the ideals of his Jewish heritage, he has always aspired to be a scholar rather than a tradesman. Though he is well-intentioned toward others, his personal life has become chaotic. To assuage his loneliness after the death of his family, he started an affair with the married twin sister of his deceased wife. They meet regularly and discreetly for their lovemaking but are otherwise in contact, rather awkwardly, as friends and family members. Their relationship is obviously too fraught with family complications to have much future. Mr. Edelman is a man of considerable charm, for even his widowed daughter-in-law prop-

ositions him. He politely rejects her rather melancholy advances.
Now the empty life of this kindhearted, serious-minded man will
be filled in a more healthy way by the child. When he looks at
Minnie he does not see a homely, unwanted child, as her parents
do. Instead, he pronounces her a marvelous baby.

When Maddy tells her mother that she is giving Minnie to Mr.
Edelman, she expects recriminations. Instead, to her surprise, her
mother is delighted. Mother's notion of Jews is that they are good
parents, have lots of money, and value education. Minnie's grandmother, curiously, has no concern that her grandchild will not
receive a Roman Catholic religious upbringing. Quite satisfied
herself, she manages to convince Maddy that giving her baby
away to such a distinguished man is an altruistic act. Waxing
eloquent, Maddy's mother envisions the luxurious life the baby
will lead, the splendid toys she will have—giant stuffed animals,
elegant dolls, her own enormous room filled with the art objects
that give a young girl pleasure. Warming to her subject, Maddy's
mother describes the college education Minnie will certainly be
given. Again she reminds Maddy that Jews, as everyone knows,
care about two things: money and education. "They become bank-
ers or teachers. They read books—not magazines—at night."

The narrative becomes a bit cluttered, as it moves toward its
denouement. While Mr. Edelman and Minnie leave for a new life
in Florida, Jed and Maddy, even without their baby, cannot sal-
vage their marriage. They part company. Jed drifts away to an
uncertain future, while Maddy goes west where, assisted by an
older sister who is an airline stewardess, she lands a job as a
ticket agent.

The reader is left with no doubt that the child will have the
best life Mr. Edelman can offer. More important, Minnie will be
loved. It would be interesting, if Norma Klein were more given
to the writing of sequels, to have a further book that followed the
adventures of man and child in Florida. Mr. Edelman, who has
ideals and good instincts, is very unlikely to turn into a father
like Capri's, whose notion of parenting is the heaping of material
benefits on his offspring. It is almost certain that Minnie (provided
she chooses at the accountable age to convert to the religion of

her adoptive father) will develop into a Jewish woman of character and compassion rather than a Jewish-American Princess.

The contrast between Maddy and Capri remains one of the most interesting features of *The Swap*. Neither young woman behaves especially well. Maddy is not liberated. She has had only high school courses and initially has no ambitions beyond a life as a beautician and housewife. By the end of the book, however, her expectations have risen considerably. The virtues of hard work will serve her well, and she will probably make a second marriage that is better than her first. Yet it is hard to respect her attempts at motherhood and the ease with which she has disposed of her firstborn child, offering it first to one person and then another. Capri, on the other hand, has had every privilege. She is bright and fully expects a lucrative career, perhaps in medicine, following her father's calling. She is equally certain of an advantageous marriage. So self-confident is Capri that she is even able to make Jed feel momentarily ambitious, and certainly discontent in his life with Maddy. Capri is, ironically, enthusiastic about Women's Studies, and contemplates—though at considerable distance from grim reality—women's problems and issues. Maddy actually lives them. In her blithe affair with Maddy's husband, Capri shows not the slightest hint of sisterhood sympathies. She is totally selfish, using men and sexuality as a pastime, her cushion against boredom.

Maddy, meanwhile, works part-time in a beauty shop, where the daily routine includes watching the soap opera "General Hospital." The working-class women who frequent the shop appear to make life decisions based on the lessons they learn from the drama. On the other hand, the college girls such as Capri who patronize the shop consider the program great camp, hooting at it, and making fun of its actors.

The working-class women have a Hollywood-inspired belief in the importance of a woman's good looks. This is to be expected; nobody has raised their consciousness. Yet Capri too—who likes to let people know that she was romantically begotten on the Isle of Capri—is also very much aware of her striking beauty and the benefits to be derived from it. While the working-class women can only look forward to lives of routine tedium, Capri, despite her opportunities, seems equally destined to a superficial existence ultimately no richer than theirs. Relationships for her are likely to be no more than a series of games or manipulations, not unlike soap opera episodes.

In these books Klein has successfully shown a number of different family styles. Unmarried women and lesbians may be good parents; so may fathers, stepfathers, and foster fathers. Even middle-aged men may hold great promise as the single parents of adopted children. Nevertheless, the value of family life is as apparent in Klein stories as in the fiction it revolts against, the sentimental, genteel tales that perpetuated the traditions of Victorian childhood. The home is still the fortress against the world, and family (though not necessarily biological kin) are the people who can be depended on. They are the ones who will nurture. Ultimately, with her own twists and reversals, Norma Klein remains as pro-family as any member of the Moral Majority.

7. The Literary Psychologist: Different Ways of Hiding

One feature of Norma Klein's work, perhaps her very strongest, has received relatively little attention. This is the informed and balanced use of psychology that has enhanced her fiction from the beginning. As the favored child of a New York psychiatrist, Klein comes by this skill honestly. Though the awareness of the complexities of human psychology is evident in almost everything she has written, two of her strongest books, *Hiding* and *Angel Face,* are especially revealing when examined as psychological studies in fiction.

Hiding was published in 1976. Today Klein describes it as a book that has "fallen between the cracks, disappeared." She claims to hardly remember it herself. The disappearance of *Hiding* is indeed unfortunate, because it is a minor masterpiece, not only one of the finest books Klein has written but one of the strongest to be found in contemporary young adult fiction. It is almost certainly not by design that *Hiding* bears a stylistic resemblance to the fiction of Alain Robbe-Grillet and Albert Camus, two French writers especially alert to the importance of language as a vehicle for communicating a particular angle of vision. The stylistic sophistication of *Hiding* may in fact be one of the factors inhibiting the popular acceptance of the book. Because of its special intricacies, *Hiding* may always be admired more by mature students of literature than by the young for whom it was chiefly written. Klein's average young reader may actually be disturbed, not so much by what happens in the narrative as by the way the happenings are related at an unfamiliar low pitch that accurately mirrors the depressed mental state of the heroine-narrator.

Even before events begin to unfold the book's simple, efficient prose helps characterize the first-person narrator, Krii. She is eighteen, weighs only ninety-eight pounds, and is described by her family as "frail," "fragile," and "a pale, shrinking little thing." Others speak of her more generously as "the ethereal type." Though Krii hovers on the brink of serious mental illness, she is nevertheless a keen observer with considerable insight. The narrative style, without ornamentation, remains low-key and somewhat static, just right for this narrator.

When compared with Albert Camus's *The Stranger,* also the first-person narrative of a neurotically desensitized person who has become a detached observer of his own life, the special skill of *Hiding* is evident. The sensibility, still, is that of a teenage girl, on the edges of both adulthood and madness, who finds herself psychologically lost in a foreign land, unable to cope with her family, her developing sexuality, and her own talents. Literary form and content are here brilliantly united.

Those readers who have throughout the years complained of a lack of real action in Klein novels will find in *Hiding* even less external plotting than usual. Krii, a shy American girl, relates her experiences during a period of ballet study in England. Throughout this time, though she often seems to be watching herself from a great distance, she undergoes the most traumatic coming-of-age rites—courtship and seduction. Socially and sexually inhibited, she is still wooed by Jonathan, an attractive young choreographer in the ballet company where she is studying and performing. Almost without realizing it, and certainly without understanding her own feelings, she begins to respond to him. In the meantime, he has interpreted her reticence as a lack of interest; half in spite, he marries a more aggressive and outwardly successful American ballet student. When he later tries to explain his hasty action to Krii, his ardent confession gives her satisfaction, even though she is alert enough to realize he is not telling the whole truth.

Krii does not fully understand either her own or Jonathan's motivations. She responds to his marriage by leaving ballet school, going to her parents' home in England, and hiding out for several days in their attic. Unseen by the family, she observes their comings and goings. Food presents no problem: she has never been a meat-eater (having always identified with animals), and she has rarely ever eaten balanced meals. When the family is asleep at night, she comes out of hiding, like an insect, and raids the refrigerator. She remains alone in the family attic for almost a week. Having always enjoyed solitude and admittedly something of a voyeur, she prefers observing the lives of others to participating in them. While in the attic, she entertains herself by playacting and dressing in the costumes she finds there. She even finds the wedding dress of the grandmother for whom she was named.

There is time during her hiding for some serious reflection. Krii perceives that she could easily lose her will to leave the attic, along with her sense of time. She thinks about animal existence and how it must be like this. Naturally, she also relishes the fantasy that Jonathan is distraught by her disappearance. When she thinks about her parents, her brother, and her sister, it is chiefly to recall how remote they have always seemed. Finally she does decide to come out of the attic, concluding that "one's life is one's own responsibility" and that it cannot "be dumped on anyone else." Not feeling afraid anymore, she checks into a local inn and has a lonely, lovely hot bath before officially returning home to her parents. At that point she announces her decision to leave ballet, where she concludes there is no great future for her anyhow. To the relief of her family, she further informs them of her intention to follow the more conventional life of a college student in the United States.

In the course of these events, described in only 124 pages in the paperback edition, much is learned about Krii, her irregular background, and her likely prospects for the future. Like most of Klein's narratives, this one ends hopefully, if not with total happiness for all. In the last scenes Krii is shown adjusting well to college life in a coed dorm. Jonathan's marriage is not flourishing, though he is proud of the child born of it. He comes to America in order to see Krii again. While no commitment is made, the book concludes with the strong suggestion that they, more mature for their intervening separation and confusion, may have a future.

Hiding is valuable for its authentic exploration of a psychological state that would likely be labeled "mild schizophrenia." A therapist might loosely diagnose Krii as a schizoid personality. But, as a credit to Klein's skill as a fiction writer, Krii remains a believable and well-individualized personality as well as a type of mental aberration. The very fact that her character is so consistently developed and presents such an authentic case study may be another reason the book has not been more successful with young adult audiences. Krii is simply too pathological for the average teenager to identify with her.

Krii's retreat from ballet school and her behavior after the collapse of her love affair would once have been termed a "nervous breakdown," the Victorian young woman's characteristic reaction to being jilted. Krii is frightened and disassociated, though not disturbed enough to be "commitable." A contemporary psychiatric explanation would, of course, employ different terminology. She passes out of her bad state in due time, through self-therapy, and seems to be on her way to establishing better relationships with her family than she has ever known before. Since her "breakdown" has been mild, she is able to work herself out of it. The reader is left to believe that she will be able to continue a low-stress career, quite possibly in a science laboratory such as the one where the book leaves her. She may also be able to maintain a family life with an especially understanding man much like Jonathan. While there is no certainty that she is totally cured and will never have to be hospitalized, the prognosis seems generally good.

Krii's personality disorder is so subtly revealed that, again, Klein's youthful audience may be bewildered by the very skill of this narrative. Since few will have had the training or experience to understand the sort of personality that is delineated, readers may be left with the feeling that the author is not telling all. Krii has a series of fears that a psychologist would label "hysterical." Not inappropriately for a person her age, her apprehensions are chiefly sexual. Though she comes to respond to Jonathan sexually and at the end of the story is no longer shocked when she sees men coming out of the shower in the coed college dorm where she is living, she never fully overcomes her discomfort with physical lovemaking. Her sexual as well as emotional feelings remain hazy and vague.

The one genuinely psychotic episode occurs when she hides in the attic and watches the movements of her family. Had her parents known they were being watched, especially by their daughter, they would certainly have found the experience creepy and would possibly have questioned the wisdom of allowing Krii to go away to college within a few weeks. Yet even before this episode, precipitated by Jonathan's marriage, a pattern of psychological and physical withdrawal has been clearly established. Krii constantly thinks, "I can't commit myself." She is not sure she cares about anyone, even Jonathan. After his marriage, it is hard for her to understand her reactions and her behavior. Unable to fully accept her attraction to him, the most she can admit is that being pursued by him was flattering, especially since she knew he in turn was being sought by a much more popular dancer in the ballet troupe. It is easy to understand how Jonathan interpreted her pattern of vagueness as indifference.

To a reader versed in the literature of psychoanalysis, *Hiding* reads much like a Freudian case history. It is a literary narrative of depth and skill, the account of mild adolescent psychosis as it might have been reported, through the use of many of the patient's own words, by a therapist of literary finesse, such as Freud himself. The discourse is passive and drifting, as would be expected of someone like Krii. She describes her crisis and the way she survived it, even while expressing little feeling about it. People come and go in her life. She feels, at least on the surface, little attachment to them. She regards her family as strange and somewhat troubled. "We're five individuals," she observes, "all unhappy, all separate. Not ragingly unhappy, not nervous breakdown unhappy, but apart."

She is the youngest of three children in a family where no members have ever been close. She remembers once hearing her mother confide in a friend that Krii herself, the third child, had been an accident, a mistake. Early in her own life, Krii has decided never to marry or have children. This determination, which probably will not be lasting, seems to have been encouraged by the attitude of her parents. While they have high career expectations for their son and two daughters, they have never promoted marriage for any of them. Krii's older sister, Paula, has dramatically rebelled against family standards, scandalizing her parents and siblings by marrying a man in a religious commune and having many children by him. Krii's brother is absorbed in his medical studies and seems almost as remote from his family as Krii herself. She recalls how she once had suspected him of being homosexual, though she had subsequently concluded that he was, in fact, nothing at all. While she is hiding in the attic, however, she is surprised to see her brother making ardent love to a girlfriend, forcing Krii to rethink her earlier opinions.

Because she has an American mother and a British father, Krii thinks of herself as an odd sort of "half and half." Though her parents profess a deep loyalty to one another, they have lived apart on their respective continents through most of their married life, meeting only for summers or vacations. Krii learns, to her considerable distaste, that her father has a mistress. Even though she has never been close to him or felt "especially cherished" by him, Krii prides herself on never having been a bother to her father. She admires his intelligence and feels inadequate in his presence. When by accident she meets him with his mistress, she wishes merely to avoid unpleasantness. She is highly uncomfortable when he insists she listen to his justification of his conduct, as he tries to explain that her mother has never been very sexually responsive to him.

Sexuality is always fraught with peril, as Krii sees it. She prefers not to discuss the subject, remembering from childhood a pet basset hound who died just two days after its first amorous encounter. Krii also remembers how she herself almost passed out in high school while watching a film on childbirth. After being subjected to her father's speech in defense of his taking a mistress, Krii rethinks her earlier views of marriage. Before, she had thought of herself as not good enough for marriage; now marriage itself seems such "a shoddy institution that *it* suddenly is not good enough for her." She feels sadly sophisticated, reminding herself of a character in a Françoise Sagan novel.

Krii also disassociates herself from her own body. She dislikes it, finding it too short for dancing and not of much worth for anything else. When she first makes love with Jonathan, she views herself, as it were, from a considerable distance. For reasons she never fully understands, she describes the experience as "painful . . . but not hideous, . . . I didn't hemorrhage, à la Sylvia Plath or want to scream aloud. I was glad of the pain actually, because it gave me an excuse not to have to worry about not feeling pleasure. Of course, I know that can't last, but I intend to hang on to such excuses as long as I possibly can."

Other people find Krii interesting or romantic in appearance, with her flowing hair and red velvet Victorian skirts. She is aptly, if cattily, described by the other girls in her dancing troupe as "Opheliaesque."

Another mark of her disassociation is Krii's likening of herself to a figure in a Chagall painting, floating about, sailing over rooftops. She further compares herself to animals, musing: "Animals really are lucky. Their physical presence is considered enough. No one says to them: 'Talk, share your feelings, why are you so quiet?' They can just lie there, smiling enigmatically, and no one can force them to reveal what they're thinking. I'm sure their inner life is as rich as any person's, but it can remain just that—inner. Perhaps I'll be reincarnated as a cat or perhaps I was one once. I enjoy contemplating that."

It is not surprising that she loves dancing the role of animals, being in their costumes. She does not willingly give up one of her animal parts even for the opportunity to dance the human lead in a ballet. She especially likes her role as a mouse in *Sleeping*

Beauty. When she overhears others saying she has "that droopy, Opheliaish air," she thinks that "mouse-like" would be a more accurate description. Once, when she sees herself in a mirror while in costume, it is difficult for a moment to distinguish the reality from the fantasy: "when I looked up, what I saw . . . was a mouse's head, large and gray, with long, painted whiskers and my own eyes, only dimly visible, through the lids."

She reflects that the pronoun *I* scares her; she has never liked first-person composition at school. In fact, she has been drawn to the stage because there, covered by costumes that sometimes even change her species, she can shed her identity. She contemplates herself as she would like to appear in, say, group scenes from a play: "if I think of myself, I imagine myself as a chair in the corner of the room; or a window shade, or a cat sleeping in the sun: present, but not necessarily the center of the action."

When Krii faces her major crisis—the marriage of Jonathan and the accumulation of family worries—she again thinks of animals. She consciously compares herself to those small defenseless animals who know when to hide and are wise rather than cowardly when they refuse to take on big animals.

The consistency of characterization and narrative tone are among the strengths of Klein's story of alienation. In the very beginning, Krii says that she has never lived in a house; home has always been an apartment. She never has had roots or felt that she really belonged to any place or person. Though her father is British and she knows the country well, she feels foreign in England. Yet, she has rather liked being a foreigner; in England her oddity is not observed, as it would be at home. She feels, like Hamlet, sent to England where everyone else is so mad that individual madness will go unnoticed. At home in the United States Krii had never belonged, even at Fenton, her private school, which prided itself on encouraging individualism. Ballet classes were even then an escape, where she was permitted to be eccentric in the name of art.

Jonathan is intrigued by Krii's wistfulness and shyness, which he interprets as a poetic aloneness. It is not on principle that she at first resists an affair. She has no strong feelings about the moral status of "relationships"; she is just embarrassed to be seen even kissing him. Jonathan gives her a friendship ring, and she fears that now others will know. At Fenton Krii had had no experience with sex, and she had resisted discussing the subject even with her mother. While Mother liked to think of herself as liberal, Krii discovered very quickly how ill-at-ease she was with sexual matters. In her desire to be calm Mother had always made sex seem so matter-of-fact it became uninteresting.

One reason Krii gives for accepting Jonathan, after hesitation, is that she has come to consider her virginity a burden. Only really passionate girls, she reasons with some perception, make good virgins. She is obviously not in that category. Virginity is merely a state she wishes to put behind her. The bisexual dancers in her ballet company are especially troubling to her. She thinks to herself: "Anything but THAT! . . . Imagine having to feel vulnerable about the entire human race. I can't imagine anything worse."

Krii's pattern of retreat is established early. Near the beginning of her narrative she observes: "Clearly, sexual relationships are not going to be my forte in life, which is a pity. It would be nice to be like that French actress I saw in a movie just before I left the States. She was dark and poised and witty and lived alone and had affairs 'like a man.' I do admire that kind of woman, especially since I'll never even be in the running for the other . . . hearty, warm, big-breasted, maternal Liv Ullmann kind."

Jonathan laments that when they make love Krii seems a million miles away. Though he is complaining, she knows that he is really intrigued by her aloofness. She recognizes that her frigidity is a challenge to men. When Jonathan does marry, he is not merely on the rebound but, nearing thirty, he seriously wants to establish a family. Krii in part feels relief, "in spite of being brokenhearted." She reminds herself that she has always enjoyed solitude and will be a better daydreamer than a wife.

Though she sleeps with the married Jonathan once, the experience is physically and emotionally frustrating and leaves her in tears. Her life has been designed to avoid scenes, and she has trained herself to hide at the first sign of conflict. This is what she will now do. Jonathan tries to reassure her, telling her not to fear her sexual nature. He tells her there is no reason for her constantly to hide in her long dresses, with her flowing hair obscuring her face. People are always asking her to remove her mask, but she realizes how vulnerable her naked countenance would be.

Krii is well aware of the way others view her. She knows that when Jonathan visits her in the middle of the night he thinks of her as a creature from the nineteenth century, with her romantically disheveled hair and her white nightgown. He admits to her that his wife thinks she is crazy, but he obviously remains entranced. Jonathan himself has been no stranger to mental illness. His own mother has been one of those women with mangled, obsessive lives of misfortune.

Though her experiences have been painful, Krii has also reached some understanding of the potential danger of her psychological state, recognizing her "capacity to disintegrate" and likening it to a precancerous state. At the end of her narrative there are signs that she is getting her life together in earnest, though her emotional equilibrium will perhaps always be precarious. Her father is surprised by the sudden vehemence of the opinions she expresses—coming from this little family mouse—and by her budding feminism. For example, she takes issue with his attitude toward his mistress, whom he has commended for having "a certain charm, a certain intelligence without aggression." This, Krii concludes, is a description of a convenience rather than a person.

Krii's decision to leave ballet, a dead end for her, and return to the United States also shows her new maturity and rationality. Though she has some talent as a dancer, she now realizes that she is physically too small for a successful career. She is now able to acknowledge that her reasons for choosing dance were personal and neurotic rather than artistic. Her parents have always wanted her to attend college, and they show their delight when she is accepted at Barnard. She concludes that it no longer makes sense to resist their ambitions for her education.

When Jonathan turns up somewhat later in the United States, he finds her significantly changed. She has decided to major in science and is hard at work in her white lab coat, wearing tortoise-shell glasses, with her hair in a ponytail. She complains to him that with her new glasses she sees things all too clearly and is not sure whether she really wants this sort of perception. She has, of course, always asserted that she is not so dense as people usually think.

Not only does Krii appear to be taking charge of her life, but her entire family seems to be moving—though in a direction that begins to strain credulity—toward one of those conventional Klein Hollywood happy endings. The parents express some desire for a more conventional married life and are actually planning to live together on a permanent basis. Older sister Paula leaves her commune and has an abortion instead of another baby. In keeping with their liberal philosophy, the family members interpret Paula's actions as a healthy sign. Krii's older brother is by now seriously courting his girlfriend and will probably marry her. Jonathan will end his hasty, thoughtless marriage and will probably become reconciled with Krii. Thus concludes this otherwise highly satisfactory and skillful book—not too convincingly.

Klein's other outstanding psychological study of recent years, possibly the richest book to date, is *Angel Face,* which appeared in 1984. Since Klein fought hard to maintain the integrity of its ending—young adult books are not supposed to end with death—it seems particularly ironic that she was chastized by some reviewers. Critiques of the book, in fact, were rather harsh. Elizabeth D. and Ben F. Nelms mentioned *Angel Face* unfavorably in an article that examined young adult fiction in general. They concluded that the book "sets a low standard for this genre." The Nelmses found the entire book distasteful, and felt it was especially demeaning to teenage boys. They described Jason, the protagonist, as single-mindedly questing for narcissistic sexual gratification. That he did not attain his goal was of little matter, according to the Nelmses, because he was "such an unpleasant character it's hard to see how readers can sympathize with him."

The Nelmses found the other characters of the book no more appealing than Jason. They described Fay, his mother, as "foul-mouthed and bitter," while his father was pronounced an overaged adolescent experiencing his own sexual liberation for the first time. The Nelmses were obviously disturbed by Klein's failure to write a book of advice that would assist young people in their sexual coming-of-age. The criticism was thus primarily ethical rather than literary, like so much that continues to pass for literary analysis in the adolescent field.[1]

Other critics were slightly more favorable, praising Klein's usual candor, her lively dialogue, and the genuine pathos she injected into the narrative, though some reviewers found the book cluttered with too many emotional problems. Each character seemed to have enough of his or her own to generate an entire book. Some critiques pronounced the story too trendy, others too melodramatic.[2]

Whatever our judgments of the quality of the book, several features of *Angel Face* deserve particular attention. It is unlike Klein's typical adolescent romance in several ways. An adolescent male, rather than the more usual teenage female of the earlier Klein romances, is its central character and first-person narrator. Jason Lieberman modestly presents himself as an anti-hero, a bit of a "pothead" who is a failure in school and a bumbler whose love life never rises above what he calls his "X-rated fantasies."

Yet, despite Jason's accounting of himself, the careful reader who is not searching primarily for an adolescent morality fable soon learns that Jason has both personality and character. During the crisis he relates, he changes, grows, and matures, so that he emerges as not only one of the liveliest and most believable characters Klein has created but also one of the most likable. The portrait of Jason is, furthermore, another of the strongest psychological studies in contemporary adolescent fiction.

The book records the efforts of this troubled and sensitive young man to make the psychological and moral transition from childhood to maturity. Though Jason's psychological troubles are not so severe as Krii's, his family turmoil is much greater.

A *Bildungsroman* of considerable power, *Angel Face* may be placed without absurdity within a tradition that includes writings by Samuel Butler, Charles Dickens, and Somerset Maugham. Just because the young man is a somewhat more affluent American does not mean his problems are experienced less painfully than those of the characters in the European "coming-of-age" story. As a novelist of male adolescent discovery, Klein is also entitled to comparison with other American writers known for their young male heroes: Mark Twain, Sherwood Anderson, Booth Tarkington, J. D. Salinger, and Philip Roth. Few other American women have written this type of fiction so successfully. Jason, Klein's hero, like Huckleberry Finn, Holden Caulfield, and Alexander Portnoy, must divest himself of family, submit to American rites of initiation, more subtle than those of primitive societies but as essential, and undergo a physical odyssey as well as a spiritual quest. He is faced with parents, however well-meaning, who are no less devastatingly inhibiting than those that encumbered Finn, Caulfield, and Portnoy.

Angel Face differs further from the customary Klein novel in that it does not provide a pat, happy resolution to all the conflicts introduced. In fact, there is some justification for the criticism that the conflicts get out of hand; the reader must mentally juggle so much turmoil that a diagram becomes almost necessary to keep up with which character is wrestling with which particular problem.

Jason's mother, Fay, is the most interesting character in the book, and her death is experienced in its full poignancy—too painfully, Klein's editors initially felt, for a teenage book. Yet this death is the event that forces Jason to rethink his life, accept responsibility for himself and others, and move more courageously into manhood.

Sexual discovery is also a central and significant theme of the book. Jason envies his older brother Ty, who is successful in wooing his skating partner, Juliet. Jason fears that no woman will ever find him acceptable as a sexual partner. In a world where beings seem to go in pairs, Jason sees himself as odd man out. From the sidelines, and with mixed emotions, he observes his father's love for Randy, the woman who becomes his stepmother. He perceives that his sister's affair with a married man, though certain to come to no good end, has at least given some temporary meaning to her life. His best friend, Otis, has heated assignations with a coed, Marcella. Even his favorite teacher, Ms. Korbel, one of the few adults who has respected and tried to understand him, is getting married.

When Vicki, an attractive classmate, seeks him out, Jason is awkward and uncertain. All year long he dreams of fully consummating their relationship, but when she is finally ready and suggests he share her sleeping bag during a camping trip, it is too late. His depression over his mother's death has sapped his erotic energies. Instead of making love to Vicki, he totals his father's car while taking her home. He is still technically—and perhaps even spiritually—a virgin at the end of the book, and he has learned that life demands to be taken seriously. He acknowledges that his search is no longer merely for pleasurable sensations.

In brief, *Angel Face* is the account of a milestone year in the lives of the six members of the Lieberman family. Jason reacts to the breakup of his parents' marriage, his father's second marriage, and his mother's sudden death in what may be interpreted officially as an automobile accident but was almost certainly suicide. Against this background of general family turmoil, his two sisters, Andy and Erin, and his brother, Ty, must each struggle with personal crises.

While the Liebermans share the upper middle-class values of most Klein characters, they have constant financial worries. The children have not attended the best schools nor had all the advantages American youth of their class have come to expect. Only Erin, who has suffered from both dyslexia and anorexia, is sent to a private school, at considerable family sacrifice. Because of her superior intelligence, Andy, the oldest sibling, has earned scholarships at Princeton and Harvard Law School. While Mort, the father, is diligent and capable, he has always been more idealistic than pragmatic in his vocational choices. His many job shifts have left the family economically insecure, and his present position as editor of *Human Rights,* a journal supporting *all* oppressed minorities, brings other than generous monetary rewards.

One of its side benefits, however, is an introduction to Randall Wormwood Hamilton, known as Randy, a free-lance writer of Quaker sentiments, the woman he quickly falls in love with.

Fay, the mother, has felt the straitened financial circumstances most keenly. Her own father's fortune collapsed during her youth but not before she had received the benefit of a finishing school education. Her college training in twelfth-century Chinese poetry has left her ill-equipped to be anything other than a lady, and she seems temperamentally unsuited as well to earning a living.

After Fay's death, the family relocates from New York to the West Coast. Father's feelings of guilt for having left Fay, despite years of provocation to which even the children bear witness, make it impossible for him to even discuss her calmly. While Randy, as second wife, welcomes the children of the first marriage into her home and they can articulate no particular objection to her, they have difficulty really liking her. She is, they acknowledge, a modestly attractive woman who looks and acts more like a mother than a homebreaker. While her marriage to Mort will probably last and provide a measure of contentment neither has before experienced, it will be a difficult union for her. In her first year of marriage, this middle-aged, first-time bride must contend with her predecessor's death (which may even have been in part a calculated assault on her), a mentally ill stepdaughter, serious financial problems, and a weight of guilt from which no amount of rationalizing can bring total relief.

The use of a teenage first-person narrator—in this case Jason— follows the convention of the adolescent novel. Jason is an excellent choice for this role; the point of view, attitudes, and language throughout the narrative are convincingly those of a fifteen-year-old of his milieu. He tells his story directly and honestly. Though he is caught up in the family problems, he has found his own way of hiding. He cushions himself by his constant use of drugs, his "pothead" lifestyle, and his sexual fantasies. In this sad way he achieves enough objectivity to be a reliable reporter of what transpires in his family. Though Jason does not always fully understand the implications of the events he observes and reports so accurately, the reader is able to discern much more.

Only Jason is strategically positioned to fully report the action that centers on Mom, because he is the only one of the children still at home almost all the time. Andy is in college and Erin, because of her learning disability, is in boarding school. Ty, infatuated with his girlfriend and largely indifferent to what goes on in his own family, sleeps over at Juliet's house most nights. Jason, who has never been able to understand why he has always been the favorite of both his parents, is also the one child in whom Mom tries to confide. Sadly, his drug stupor and adolescent self-absorption prevent him from fully perceiving the gravity of Mom's crisis, which she covers thinly under a torrent of black humor.

Jason's own vision is opaque. After his mother's death, he is unable to acknowledge, even to himself, that he is in a state of depression. Instead, the reader notes his inability to make love to Vicki and his shadowlike presence in his stepmother's household. No explanation is given for his sudden wrecking of his father's car, but his mental state is clear to his father, who does not even complain, as well as to the reader. It is significant that Jason survives his own accident, which is so obviously an acting out of his mother's fatal crash. He is making a clear affirmation of life. Though he will not become a model student overnight, nor a model son—there is still too much hostility to Dad—he is putting his self-destructive habits slowly behind him. There will certainly be less pot smoking and fewer evasions of responsibility. He will eventually come out of hiding.

Contrast and irony are effectively used. Mother's character comes into clearer relief when Randy, the second wife, is perceived as her foil. Even the names of the two women significantly contrast. Mother's name, Fay, with its suggestions of the ephemeral and of poetic "feyness," at first appears ironic but later seems to fit. The woman who replaces her in Mort's life, Randall Wormwood Hamilton, bears a name only befitting an Episcopalian, Mom sarcastically reasons, until she learns that Randy is a Quaker, a do-gooder who is now wrecking a family. Contrasted with Randy's Quaker activism, which includes "liberating" the man she loves, is Mom's long-dead and seemingly despised Presbyterian background. While Randy is an inhibited woman, almost too controlled, Mom is a constantly vocal example of what is widely referred to as "the hysterical personality type." Her speech is lively and entertaining, even when she is feverishly composing witticisms to cover her agony; Randy's best conversation, by contrast, always remains banal. At every point, Randy's calm is contrasted with Mom's passion.

Even their physical descriptions enhance their differences. Mom is thin, nervous in mannerisms, and sometimes careless in appearance, while Randy is restrained and always neat, almost compulsively so. Her life has, if anything, been excessively ordered, while Mom's has been a chaos.

After Dad leaves, Mom self-pityingly laments that she has spent all her years cooking and cleaning rather than preparing to earn a living. Yet no member of her family remembers her doing much housekeeping, and their diet all too often has consisted of frozen dinners. Randy, on the other hand, sets about housekeeping as methodically as she has always done everything else. While Randy has earned her living from an early age as an earnest and reasonably successful free-lance journalist, Mom, with her esoteric intellectual specialties and neuroticism, remains incapable of financial independence.

The further irony, which strikes even Jason, is the contrast between Mom's vision of herself as the long-suffering, rejected wife and the reality of what her marriage has actually been. When she is able to be analytical, she admits that her marriage came about for the wrong reasons: Dad was on the rebound, and she was, she claims, ready to marry anyone who did not read *Time* or smell of garlic. Their quarrels started on their honeymoon and continued. It is no secret to the children that both Mom and Dad have had lovers. Once Dad left home for six weeks of housekeeping with a girlfriend, while Mom, on another occasion, packed the children off to a dude ranch where she was vacationing with her own paramour.

Never one to quietly endure her frustrations, Mom once conducted a mock ceremony during which she buried her wedding ring in the front yard. Jason assumes it is still there, unless the dogs have dug it up. It is by the accumulation of such details that

Klein skillfully conveys the presence of her characters and the chaotic quality of their day-to-day lives.

Klein's style in *Angel Face* is so skillful that it appears deceptively simple. Not for once is the reader tempted to believe that anyone other than a fifteen-year-old is telling the tale. The illusion of the density and texture of this particular family life is achieved by Jason's habit of allowing the characters to speak for themselves. The syntax and vocabulary convey the rhythms of real conversation in the social circle to which these people belong. Little figurative language is used; Klein does not strive for an elegaic tone. Jason is barely getting through high school. Though he is highly intelligent, he has never been identified as either a poet or a rhetorician. His narrative reflects these facts. While the rhythms and patterns of speech are neither highly distinctive nor self-conscious, they are right for the characters and events related. Despite Jason's age and psychological state, when he observes his family he reveals a practical, pragmatic strain that will serve him well, the reader knows, in the future.

Skill of characterization, above all, makes this novel one of the most successful Klein has written. The major characters all come to life. They are delineated cleanly and efficiently, first by Jason, who describes them as he perceives them, then by their own words and actions. While all members of the Lieberman family are vividly portrayed, Mom's portrait is the masterpiece.

Mom's diatribes not only characterize her but do much to establish the poignancy of the family situation. At one point, she tells Jason, before lapsing into tears, exactly what Dad's problem is:

> . . . life was supposed to be perfect. Because Mama said be a good little Jewish boy and work hard and get good grades and marry and have kids and all that shit, and he did it and it didn't work out. . . . Of course Mama *didn't* say fuck around on the side with little Quakerettes or little Catholic secretaries. I mean, listen, we have something to be thankful for, right? What if he'd married the little Catholic kid? She'd have had ten more kids before they got home from the church. This—I have to admit it—it sounds like a perfect match.

Mom is believably acknowledged to be a mass of contradictions. Jason reflects, "Mom has so many prejudices that I can't keep track of all of them, and they almost seem to cancel each other out."

It is typical of Mom that she carefully plots a Thanksgiving dinner at which she intends to calmly announce the divorce plans to the entire family. After preparing turkey and trimmings and, uncharacteristically, setting a splendid table for what she pretends is going to be a civilized family scene, she loses composure at the moment of announcement and blurts out: "He's leaving because he's found a lady he likes to fuck better than me."

Jason recalls that even in happier times holidays have been difficult in his household: "It always seemed like my parents had their worst fights around holidays, especially Christmas. Either Dad got Mom the wrong present, or once he just gave her money, saying she should buy whatever she wanted, and she said that made her feel like a whore, just finding a check on her desk. Stuff like that. Maybe all families feel that way a little. Like holidays should be this great cozy warm time and it isn't. Probably even in 'normal' families it isn't."

While Mom's personality dominates the book, Jason himself is a well-revealed character. His not unusual feelings of adolescent persecution are well brought out. Most of his high school teachers have given up on him. Brother Ty constantly humiliates him by using the childhood nickname of "Angel Face" his mother, who even then favored him, had bestowed because of his blond curls. Ty sneers that Jason constantly ogles Juliet, cannot attract a girlfriend of his own, and spends hours in his room "jerking off."

On the day all the males in his school are to dress as Rhett Butler, Jason makes a characteristic mistake, trying to recreate antebellum days by borrowing Mom's fencing sword. He makes his entrance looking like a bandit who has just emerged from Sherwood Forest, exposing himself to further ridicule. Though he narrates his failures and faults in a straightforward fashion, the reader learns more about Jason through his actions, his interactions with family and friends, and through the opinion others have of him. Ms. Korbel, the one teacher who genuinely likes him, and Vicki, the coed who seeks him out, obviously have found traits Jason has not yet credited to himself. For all his limitations, he inspires affection. His reliance on pot to help him get through the miserable days at his school and endure his family crises appears to be his way of coping—not the best way, perhaps, but the only means of emotional survival he finds at hand.

While Vicki has sensed Jason's potential manliness, Ms. Korbel has perceived his gentleness from observing him in her classroom, where he has been a far-from-distinguished student. Engaging him to "sit" with her aging father while she dates her fiancé, she demonstrates a confidence that others have lacked. His compassion is evident in the attention he gives Mr. Korbel and in his concern for his own two troubled sisters.

An oddly unresolved action, and one that appears totally out of character is Jason's theft of fifty dollars from Ms. Korbel. The money was one of her wedding gifts; with it Jason buys a pink cashmere sweater as a birthday present to impress Vicki. Though he promises himself he will replace the money, he never does, perhaps because Mom's unexpected death makes him forget all obligations, or perhaps because Klein failed to tie up all her loose narrative threads. This petty theft contributes nothing to an understanding of the personalities or themes of the book. Jason, while no paragon, has at least been honest up to this point.

Jason's siblings are also believably delineated. Ty's selfishness is revealed in his constant ridicule of his brother and in his total absorption in the shallow Juliet, to the neglect of his family in its time of need. When the impending divorce of his parents is announced at that fateful Thanksgiving dinner, all he can think about is what will be served for dessert. Though the two sisters, both away at school, appear in only a few scenes, they seem very real. Erin, who bursts into tears at the slightest provocation and can never fully accept her parents' divorce or her mother's death, reminds her family of Laura in *The Glass Menagerie*. The revealing detail that she likes drawing unicorns as gifts for her family is worth more than a page of description. Andy's brilliance has earned her enviable scholarships to those name schools that are always so important to Klein's characters. Yet her lack of common sense is evident even to Jason when he meets her lover, a man who clearly has no intention of leaving his wife for her and has just lost his job in an important law firm through inattention to duty.

Randy, the other woman, though a convincing character, is less impressively drawn than the members of the original Lieberman family. She is neither unsympathetic nor particularly endearing. A serious, idealistic spinster who is, in her early forties, discovering genuine love for the first time, she has no scruples about encouraging Mort to end a marriage most participants and observers agree has been a twenty-seven-year disaster. Though everyone affirms Randy to be a thoughtful reader of books, who thinks about issues and has convictions, her conversation never reflects this. Klein's ear, so impressive in capturing the rhythms of Mom's speech, fails when she gives Randy words. It seems unlikely also that such a woman, whom Mom prejudicially but with some accuracy has described as "tight-assed," would upon first meeting her prospective stepchildren make small talk about her loss of virginity at advanced age. Yet this is what Jason reports her as doing.

The supporting characters are considerably less convincing and interesting than the Lieberman family members. Readers have come to expect in Klein novels an amusing assortment of peripheral personalities. While the drives, motives, and traits of the Liebermans are believably and subtly revealed, the supporting players—Ty's girlfriend Juliet; Jason's best friend, a black schoolmate, Otis; Otis's girlfriend, an Italian-American, Marcella; Jason's own chum Vicki; Ms. Korbel, the schoolteacher; and Vernon, Ms. Korbel's elderly father—are little more than stock figures, designed to swell a scene or two, all too comfortably familiar and predictable in their actions and thoughts.

Otis is a black youth right out of an ethnic-pride television situation comedy. Everyone says he is highly intelligent and perceptive, yet these traits have to be taken on faith, because he spends most of his time in an activity requiring neither brains nor insight, the bedding-down of Marcella, described as a budding Sophia Loren. Marcella, an obvious stereotype, comes across as a voluptuous and not overly bright peasant whose chief talent, outside the bedroom, is Italian cookery.

Juliet is a somewhat more successful minor figure whose vacuity is not inappropriate, because that is the point of her character. It is no surprise when she finally dumps Ty, who has been tiresomely adoring of her. Her complacent, tactless mother and father, models of nouveau riche vulgarity, are created to contrast with Jason's less successful but more genuine parents. It is Vicki who, more seriously, fails to come alive as an individual. She is meant to play an important role in Jason's developing self-confidence, but her motives are so vague that she fails to be convincing. It is never fully clear why she pursues Jason, for she appears too shallow to discern the deeper levels of his admittedly gauche personality.

Ms. Korbel is potentially interesting, though she too fails to develop full dimensions. She promotes women's liberation and self-realization. Even after her marriage she remains "Ms. Korbel," and she openly discusses her mastectomy with her classes, eliciting imaginative responses from her students to her question of how they would feel about having a breast removed. The success of her teaching methods, however, remains unclear. Her declining father, Vernon, for whom Jason "babysits," is even less well defined. Klein certainly intends him to be a quaint, cute old gentleman, but he remains merely another stereotype. In fact, throughout Klein's fiction, elderly, declining men are among the least successful characters.

Yet Klein usually does not fail in the difficult task of creating strong supporting characters. Her sketches of aging women have been far better than those of elderly men. Jason's Jewish paternal grandmother, who could easily have degenerated into an ethnic stereotype, is lively and interesting, if singularly unattractive. She makes her impact by her sole appearance at Mort's wedding to Randy. She talks too much, arrogantly reminding everyone in earshot how after rearing her children she made a career for herself and a small fortune. Even at this inappropriate moment, she cannot resist damning Fay, blaming her for all Mort's shortcomings.

Angel Face relentlessly builds to its climax, the death of Fay. There is no melodrama here, no surprise for the careful reader, no showy effect for its own sake. Klein handles the death with both skill and tact. Except that Jason speaks of his mother throughout in the present tense, as if she were still alive (and this might be explained by his mental and emotional state, his sense of her continued presence in his own psyche), the reader has been well prepared. Looking back, it is evident that Mom's death was almost a dramatic necessity from the beginning. Though she could be very witty, her humor always conveyed a bitterness that expressed a fundamental self-hatred. On one occasion she jokes about serving hemlock for dessert. She refers to herself as "sarcastic, crazed, and off-the-wall." With that appraisal the entire family seems to concur. Ty dismisses her as so loony that she is best avoided. Andy, though more compassionate, still does not understand why her mother cannot "get her act together."

Even the precise nature of the death has been carefully foreshadowed. Mom's car has never been in good working order, and her inattention to its maintenance has earlier resulted in two frantic family episodes.

In addition to her other affronts, Mom faces at the end an "empty nest." Dad and Randy have married and moved to California. Her daughters remain in school. Ty refuses to live at home. Suddenly even Jason, Mom's favorite, decides to spend the summer on the West Coast to be near the vacationing Vicki. Mom is suspicious of his explanation that he will be staying with Dad and Randy merely to save money. She only perceives that they have destroyed her home and taken her children. Now, she asks, "What do they want next, my clothes?"

Mom has desperately reached out to her family, yet each member has been too consumed by his or her private problems to provide the support she demands. Though her marriage had been a trial from the beginning, it had provided an anchor. Mom had even loved Dad in her own combative style. Literally adding insult to injury, she notes that the second wedding, despite Randy's Quaker sympathies, has taken place in a synagogue. When she and Dad married a quarter of a century before, no rabbi would officiate. Mom surely realizes that times change, but feels that they seem never to change in her favor.

The pain and humiliation of losing her husband to another woman and the trauma of the midlife decline of energies are not all Mom faces. At the precise time she needs to earn her own living and finds no market for the rather odd skills she possesses, the women's movement is vociferously proclaiming that women should be out there fulfilling themselves professionally along with men.

On the last day before he leaves for the West Coast, which Mom labels "another country," Jason makes a halfhearted offer to stay with her. Though she has been pleading with him not to leave, at the last minute she recognizes her own selfishness and sends him on his way. He has a premonition of disaster when he tells her goodbye. In fact he feels so strange and terrible that the only way he can endure his cross-continental flight is to lock himself in the washroom, hiding out and smoking marijuana.

Fay's death, the narrative's central dramatic event, brings meaning, direction, and purpose to everything that has gone before and will come later in the lives of the Lieberman children. Rather than the sentimentality all too often found in books written for young adults, Klein has provided genuine pathos. She has faithfully avoided editorializing, overwriting, poeticizing, or employing a heightened style that would have played false to her readership. She has treated her readers with respect. In the areas of sex, family relationships, and death, she has not relied on stock responses but has demanded reflection from her readers. Klein, like any honest writer, leaves the impression of having thought carefully about her themes and tested them against her observation of the lives of real people similar to her fictional characters.

The Lieberman family officially collapsed during that fateful family Thanksgiving dinner at which an embarrassed Dad and an angry Mom notified their children of their impending divorce. At the end of the book, events have come full cycle. The reconstructed family has moved from the East to the West Coast. It is a year later, Mom is dead, and it is Randy, well-meaning but obviously rejected as a substitute Mom, who has prepared the turkey and trimmings. Yet this Thanksgiving meal is silent. Topics of conversation are introduced and dropped. There are too many long pauses, and not much food is consumed. Finally Randy and Dad leave for a party. The genuine family, the four children, still with their problems and various ways of trying to come to terms with Mom's death and the changes in their lives, are more united than they have been at any time during the past year. They settle down for a game of Monopoly, as appropriate a renewal rite as any.

8. New Challenges: *Going Backwards* and *Older Men*

In a provocative and scholarly *School Library Journal* essay, Roger Sutton discusses what he perceives as the failure of contemporary books for young people to be genuinely realistic. While the books available today are often described by their publishers as "honest and hard-hitting," Sutton feels they usually fall short of these claims. He agrees with an earlier discussion published in the same journal, in which Jane Abramson complains that "facile optimism and tidy solutions" are frequently presented as answers to the problems introduced in young adult fiction. Both Abramson and Sutton agree that there have been too many "last-ditch happy endings" in books that boasted of their realism.

Contemporary young adult books, observes Sutton, generally belong to the mode of "low mimetic comedy" that has characterized the teen novel, and most popular fiction as well, since the 1950s. We have light escapist stories that demand the Hollywood happy ending, even though they come to us with a few realistic trappings. Philosophically, however, they are no more realistic than they have ever been. A new literature exists that applauds its own alleged courage but still does not accept the actual world that confronts the teenager. These books, with a few exceptions, lack "ambiguity or provocation."

Though Klein's books are not mentioned in Sutton's article, the principles and observations outlined are appropriate to an examination of them. In place of the old didacticism, Klein sometimes presents a new didacticism, not unlike what Sutton describes: "Most frequently," he says, "these novels also provide prescription: pregnant girls learn their 'options,' alcoholics (and readers) find out about Alcoholics Anonymous." Klein's books, on even superficial examination, do sometimes appear to be "prescription books" with few ambiguities remaining at the end.

While teenage problem novels do provide comforting answers, Sutton reminds his readers that the best of literature, whether written for young people or adults, stirs questions. And this is precisely what Klein's finest books have always done, in contrast to her less impressive ones. In *Breaking Up* the heroine contrasts her heterosexual father with her lesbian mother and merely concludes that there are different styles of loving, while in the earlier—and far better—book, *Taking Sides,* the ambiguities of the likely lesbian relationship stimulated the reader to examine the family situation and the issues of lifestyle options and parenting it suggested. Part of the strength of *Angel Face* is that it does not provide definite answers but leaves uncertainties for the reader to ponder. Jason, through the loss of his mother, experiences what approaches the catharsis of tragedy. He is well on his way toward achieving some of the wisdom reached through suffering, which the ancients who developed tragedy as a literary form felt was sent by the gods who preside over the destinies of humans.

At the end of his *School Library Journal* discussion, Sutton's pertinent advice is: "Let us stop pretending that we are offering teenagers 'hard-hitting,' 'shattering' realism and let us stop talking about 'tragic' when we just mean sad. We don't often offer truly challenging realism to young adults, but we have talked and written ourselves into believing that it is so."[1]

Norma Klein's best work has admirably met Sutton's challenge. Though she started her career on a high note with that groundbreaking book *Mom, the Wolf Man and Me,* it is encouraging to observe that after fifteen years of prolific writing, rather than "burning out," Klein has recently written two of the most important works of her career, *Going Backwards* and *Older Men.*

Both these young adult novels are built around dilemmas for which there can be no easy solutions. Klein does not pretend that there are. These books are additionally significant because in them Klein has generously shared with her readers certain crises she admits were faced by her own family. Transmuting this particular family pain into meaningful fiction has only been possible for her in the last few years. In accomplishing this, she has met a highly personal challenge, whatever the literary judgment ultimately placed on these books. The literary merit, however, is substantial.

Going Backwards, published in 1986, fictionalizes the decline and death of Norma Klein's own grandmother, who suffered from Alzheimer's disease. The book's counterpart to Norma's father is Dr. Goldberg, except that he is a pathologist rather than a psychiatrist. The "gentle death" of the grandmother, called Gustel in the book, at the hands of her son is presented as an act of mercy, however criminal in the eyes of the law. Yet even courageous acts of mercy may not always be performed with impunity, the book suggests. In the fictional world's providence, Dr. Goldberg suffers and under the strain of his burden of conscience meets an early death. His son Charles, who narrates the story, is Norma's fictional alter ego. Like Charles, the reader is denied access to Dr. Goldberg's intimate thoughts, but they are suggested obliquely. Family life is not the same after Gustel's death, and one episode is especially revealing. Shortly after the funeral, Mrs. Goldberg gives her husband's niece and her black maid, Josie, permission to divide up Grandmother's possessions. That family members and intimates, rather than a charitable organization, should have the dead woman's personal belongings is reasonable. Normally Dr. Goldberg is a reasonable and generous man, who has always taken Josie's part even against Grandmother's demented accusations. But the sight of his self-centered niece and the maid gleefully taking possession of his mother's clothing is more than he can endure. He angrily orders them out of the dead woman's room.

The Goldbergs are a loving family, despite an assortment of tensions, resulting chiefly from the adolescence of Charles and the sibling rivalry between Charles and his more gifted younger brother, Kaylo. The boys have caring parents, though the reader enters the family scene at the moment Dr. and Mrs. Goldberg are faced with a problem of genuine magnitude. Mom, who runs a moderately successful catering business, often seems out of touch and oblivious to the struggles of her sons. The problem with Grandmother, however, is immediate and cannot be ignored.

Gustel's present decline seems genuinely tragic, because she was once a capable, energetic woman who, despite the disadvantage of being an immigrant from Eastern Europe, was able to earn a sound living in the United States as a masseuse and provide her son with a professional education. Now she is only the hull of her former self, her mind slowly dissolving with her affliction. Her grandsons, who used to visit her in Florida, find her present personality hard to reconcile with their memory of a lively grandmother who loved playing tennis and searching for seashells on the beach. Now Gustel, who must be watched and protected, is being cared for by her son in the family apartment. Although he is devoted to her and feels he owes her a great debt for her many sacrifices, her care is far from easy. She frightens her grandsons with her nightly prowls about the apartment; she forgets where she is and even the name of her son; and she hurls racist insults at Josie, who is not only the family housekeeper but is in essence also a family member. At one point Gustel starts writing what she calls her memoirs, in Hebrew caligraphy, on the closet wall of Kaylo's room. She even comes to the dinner table partially clothed.

Finally, Dr. Goldberg bows to pressure from his wife and sons and agrees that his mother must be committed to a nursing home. The generous supply of Valium he habitually gives his mother is now no longer adequate to restrain her. He asks Charles to go with him on an inspection tour of a nearby nursing home, which he knows is the most adequate one available. Though father and son try to put the best face on what they see there, it is evident that the home is both understaffed and underequipped, humiliating to its residents and depressing to their relatives. As distasteful as the nursing home is to Dr. Goldberg, he realizes that he may lose his own immediate family if he insists they live any longer under the same roof as the mentally incapacitated Gustel.

On the eve of her commitment to the home, Gustel dies suddenly and peacefully in her sleep.

Against the backdrop of family confusion and real tragedy for his father, Charles must contend with his own adolescent insecurities. He regards himself as physically unattractive as well as gauche with girls. His father, perhaps as a less-than-kind comic relief from his own tensions, is not above needling him about his lack of experience with the opposite sex. Dad claims that he was already successful with women when he was Charles's age. His son begins to fear that he will never be able to attract a woman. Meanwhile, Mom continues to be out of touch with his struggles to achieve some semblance of manhood, absorbed in her career and her difficulties with Gustel. Only with the maid Josie does Charles experience warmth without stress. Josie is further able, with her good sense and honest compliments, to reassure him that he is not totally hopeless as a man.

After Gustel's death, Charles goes away to the university. It is here, through the reassurance of his new girlfriend, Lorraine, that he begins to develop self-confidence. It must not be too surprising for his family to later discover that Lorraine is black. In this book of oedipal undercurrents, it seems evident that the genuine maternal imprinting on Charles's consciousness has come from Josie. Fortunately, the family is lacking in race prejudice. Charles may reasonably hope for a future with Lorraine, with family approval, if the relationship continues and matures.

The smooth flow of campus life is interrupted for Charles when he is abruptly summoned home from college by the sudden death of his own father. Only after Dad has been buried does Charles learn from his mother the truth of Gustel's death. Rather than commit her to the cold hands of strangers at the nursing home, Father used his medical knowledge and access to drugs, giving her a lethal injection so that she could die peacefully in her sleep. Charles acknowledges that he is not surprised to learn that his father provided Grandmother with "the happy death." At some level of consciousness he realized it all along. The reader, too, is not surprised.

Going Backwards has considerable literary power. As usual, Klein is especially good with dialogue, characterizing the individual personalities and conveying the dynamics of Goldberg family life through conversations. Even Gustel's illness is revealed convincingly in her speech. The lively, affectionate banter between Charles and Josie is especially crucial to plot and theme. Though no attempt is made to reproduce any recognizable "black" dialects, as always, Klein is convincing when she creates dialogue for Charles and Josie. The conversational rhythms of their give-and-take are sufficiently realistic in themselves without added dialectal inflections.

Several characterizations are particularly strong. The portrait of Gustel, the once proud and able Jewish immigrant woman now ravaged by Alzheimer's disease, is skilled. Her actions are grotesquely comic, despite their pathos. Dad is also a vivid personality; a successful pathologist who has never sought wealth, he is in clumsy physical condition, lacking in glamour but strong on character. While Josie and her ex-husband, Hobart, who drives a Cadillac and spends his wife's money, may strike some readers as stereotypes, they are also people one might well meet in Manhattan. Josie is no comic black maid, but a woman capable at her job and a family friend who is strong, intelligent, and supportive. If her role in the family is like that of "black mammies" or trusted family confidantes that have appeared many times in southern writing, she is no less believable as a character.

Foils, which throw the Goldberg family members into sharp relief, are introduced throughout the book. Charles's best friend is Kim, a Korean-American youth, who may be the real stereotype in the book. Kim's parents have been successful with their fruit stands, while his sister attends MIT. The children of the family are the sort of superachievers that Klein has identified elsewhere as the young people now getting the high school science prizes that once went to Jewish youth. Kim himself will eventually attend Harvard, which Charles's erratic grades have kept out of his reach. An elderly, almost blind grandfather lives with Kim's family. He, like Gustel, is an immigrant, a survivor in America from another ancient and picturesque culture. Unlike Gustel, Kim's grandfather retains his active mind, fondly remembering life in Korea, while enjoying the benefits of the United States as well. His sudden, peaceful death in his sleep, following an afternoon excursion to the zoo with the young people, foreshadows the more complicated death of Gustel.

The controversial subject of euthanasia is tastefully handled. Klein's authorial voice does not pass intrusive judgment on Dad's painful act of humanity and conscience, though the conversations and actions of Charles and his mother indicate their general approval of Dad's decision. Yet Dr. Goldberg is tormented by guilt and is as surely punished as he would have been in a Victorian novel. Even while his reason tells him he has done right, his inescapable guilt clearly drives him to an early death. Charles dimly perceives his father's feelings, though he does not know all the reasons for them until after his death. He remembers the sudden tirades and the little scenes, so seemingly out of keeping with his father's character.

In their last discussion of Gustel, Mrs. Goldberg shares another family secret with Charles. She tells him how her own mother requested sleeping pills while she was dying of cancer. The family complied with the request of the suffering woman, leaving a generous supply on her bedside table. Her fatal overdose was taken as expected. Mom tells Charles she will want the same consideration if she is ever dying of a painful, incurable disease. Charles silently doubts he will ever be able to perform such an act of fatal mercy if Mom be the afflicted one.

There is inescapably a stark tone to sections of the book. Both Gustel and Dad are given the simplest of burials, without the presence of friends or the comforting rites of religion. In a symbolic action, Charles lifts the lid of his father's coffin, which has remained firmly closed by family request. He discovers that the body has started to decompose. With none of the customary rituals that help to assuage sorrow when a family member dies, the remaining Goldbergs must nevertheless get on with their lives.

In this novel Klein has told another tale that lingers poignantly in the memory. It is no doubt her treatment of family sorrow and courageous if harsh decision making that has given several of her books an enduring strength. *Going Backwards* is necessarily a provoking if not disturbing book. It is basically an existentialist novel, in a fictional genre rarely called upon to bear the weight of such a grim vision of reality. Dr. Goldberg has bravely, though painfully and ultimately with inescapable consequences to himself, made his choices, in a universe indifferent to human suffering. There is no deity in this universe concerned enough with human affairs to pass judgment on the hubris that leads one man to decide when another human being, even the one who has given him life, lives or dies. Yet it is conscience, that most terrible, primordial, and irrational judge, that still calls this man to account for his violation of the life principle. Reason alone would seem to amply justify, even condone, the act committed, but conscience is inexorable, inflicting a guilt quite apart from situation and circumstance.

Going Backwards ends with a cozy family scene, as necessary to the young adult family story as is the predictable marriage at the end of a comedy. Charles and his mother reassure one another that father did what he had to do. They remember how out of condition he was, how his doctor had warned him to stop smoking. His death, they both emphasize, was hardly surprising. Perhaps Charles realizes that they protest too much. He drifts off into a daydream, the familiar refuge for individuals with problems they cannot solve. In his dream, the world is nicely rearranged. He sees himself the husband of Lorraine and the father of two happy children. Dad and Grandmother, healthy and vivacious, are there along with the still-living members of the family. The dream further incorporates an impossible yearning often expressed to him by Josie, to own a farm and live in bucolic simplicity off the richness of the earth. Closing on this escapist note, the book remains wistful and consistent with its basic vision of human existence. It pronounces no definitive judgment and does not presume to present absolute solutions where there can be none.

Older Men (1987) continues Klein's sensitive use of personal family situations and relationships. This time she is coming to grips through her fiction with her often acknowledged attachment to her deceased father. The narrative is quite long for a young adult book, running 228 pages. Though it lacks both the humor and the pathetic force of *Going Backwards,* it is a serious attempt to explore problematic family issues in a manner that does not suggest easy solutions. If it does not have the impact of the earlier book, it is probably because Klein fails to fully explore the classic Electra complex she sets up in the beginning of the narrative. Instead, she sends her protagonist, Elise, on a sexual exploration not unlike that of numerous less interesting heroines of her earlier fiction. Elise's later attachment to her stepbrother, only a few years older than she, just never seems as powerful as her sad and betrayed passion for her father. Though she is aware that she sleeps with her stepbrother in large part because she knows her father would be outraged if only he knew, Elise is never quite able, perhaps because her own motivations lack clear direction, to make the cuckhold she desires of her father. While the three central members of the Dintenfass family—Elise, the daughter; June, the mother; and Nate, the father—are certainly among the more compelling characters Klein has thus far introduced, the intricacies of their relationships are never fully worked out to the reader's satisfaction.

Elise is sixteen years old. To most observers she appears to be a brainy young woman who lacks glamour, is slightly overweight, and has unruly hair along with imperfect skin. But to her father, a distinguished cardiologist and medical professor, she is a figure of nineteenth-century romance. He constantly compares her to heroines of fiction and opera, to Mozart's Queen of the Night, Bizet's Carmen, and Tolstoy's Anna Karenina. Nate delights in taking his daughter on excursions, treating her to gourmet foods, and sharing the finest pleasures of art and culture with her. He does nothing by halves; when she admires a scarf in a boutique window, he insists on buying her a sample of every scarf in the shop.

June, Elise's mother, has been depressed for many years. Her daughter has been only dimly aware of the reasons, understanding that there is both family jealousy and guilt preying upon her. She knows that her closeness to her father has made June feel rejected, as if she were an alien in her own family circle. Elise also knows that her mother married her father for the wrong reasons. At the time of her marriage, June was already expecting Elise, and she was responsible for Nate's leaving his first wife and three stepchildren. Now retribution seems to have fallen on June. Her husband has long ago lost interest in her and makes it clear that he stays with her only because he cannot bear to risk losing custody of his daughter. When June's jealous behavior becomes extreme, Nate welcomes the opportunity to commit her to an institution, where he assures everyone she will be properly treated for her "nervous breakdown." It is, however, obvious that Nate now believes there will be fewer distractions from his central preoccupation, his daughter Elise.

Elise, however, turns out to have a maturity and insight few of her friends and family would have expected. She intuitively perceives that institutionalization is not the solution for her mother, that June must declare her independence from her husband and find a residence and life of her own. Elise further realizes that she too will be caught in her father's web unless she is able to make her own escape. She acknowledges the temptation to exist in his shadow, choosing every boyfriend, lover, or even husband in an effort to recapture his image, make him jealous, or avenge herself on him for anything less than total devotion.

While her mother is in the hospital, Elise gets a job in a feminist bookstore. There she meets Kara, her father's stepdaughter from his first marriage. She not only makes friends with the older woman but mixes her blood with Kara's in a ceremony they design in order to become "blood sisters." Elise listens to the sad tale of Kara's own attachment to Nate, how he deserted her and her mother for his new family, and how Kara later made a bad marriage to an older man, in a symbolic attempt to recover him. Kara introduces Elise to her brother Tim, a not-very-successful young man who has had mental and emotional problems and still smarts from his own feelings of rejection by Nate. When Elise starts an affair with him, it is for several reasons. She finds him sensitive;

she has a typical adolescent curiosity about sex; and, even though she does not totally understand this third and most significant motivation, she finds him a surrogate for her father. Her best lovemaking takes place in her father's own house while he, unaware that she is with Tim, sleeps a short distance away.

Realizing that she is also struggling for her emotional freedom and integrity as an individual, Elise helps her mother escape from the mental institution and set up her own apartment. Though she leaves home to attend Yale, Elise does not immediately make any close friends. As she takes her own steps toward independence, she is still tormented by jealousy. When her father comes to visit bringing a new woman whose four-year-old daughter he obviously adores, she recognizes that Nate can only be happy in loving little girls. When they become women, they are no longer his innocent and pliant darlings, and are then subject to his repudiation. She tries to analyze her own feelings of betrayal: "I felt as though he had gotten divorced not only from my mother but from me as well. Yet, like many things long feared, it was less painful than I'd thought it would be. I still love him, but not with that childish, blind love I'd always had before."

June herself may remind the loyal Klein reader of Fay, the mother in *Angel Face*. Unlike Fay, June does not die but shows some promise of moving beyond her neuroses. She is fortunate in having a child sensitive to her problems and wise enough to assist her in leaving an intolerable situation. Elise refuses any longer to be caught in the middle of her parents' quarrels, and she decides she will no longer allow herself to be the unacknowledged cause of most of them. When June, in a jealous rage, accuses both Elise and her father of wanting to put her away so they will be alone together, Elise is understanding rather than angry. Though June's insinuations of incest are unfair, there are one or two scenes of unspoken sexual tension between father and daughter.

Even without the support of a competent mother, Elise is able to liberate herself from her father's smothering devotion. She insists on going to live with her grandmother rather than remain alone with her father in his apartment. While working in the feminist bookstore, she gains further sophistication reading about women like Margaret Mead and Colette who led free, active lives. Mead and Colette fascinate her because they are so unlike her mother or herself. "They crashed into life," she reflects, "breaking rules, doing whatever they wanted. I suppose some people hated them, but I admire them, having love affairs with people of both sexes, inventing life as though it were a game where you could determine the rules."

There are harshly realistic descriptions of mental hospitals in *Going Backwards,* and Klein's regular readers may find the distaste for psychiatry that the book expresses surprising. The disillusionment with psychiatry and those who practice it appears to come not just from the characters in the book but from the author herself. Though it is the obviously biased, yet well-experienced June who voices the opinion that the doctors in mental institutions are sicker than the patients and that there is not one among them who has any compassion, neither dramatic situation nor persuasive voice of any other character refutes the heated denunciation. Since Klein's own father was a psychoanalyst, the denunciation would appear to represent a further emotional divesture of the father.

By the end of the narrative Elise has escaped her parents' obsessive attempts to control her. She has given her mother what support and assistance she could provide, and she has maintained friendly ties with her father, though she sees him, inevitably, slipping away from her. She has experienced her first love affair and still has visits from Tim, her lover-stepbrother. Though some of the developmental tasks of adulthood have been accomplished, these transitions have not been without pain, and they remain incomplete. Elise thinks of how unlike fiction, at least unlike teenage fiction, life really is: "Sometimes people my age in books seem so false to me, so overly-naive, as though being a teenager, to whoever writes these books, is like belonging to some alien species. Especially the books for girls in which all they think about is whether boys will like them, what to wear, being popular." Elise further concludes that these heroines of books are basically dishonest to themselves and others, practicing the courtship tricks they have learned from *Seventeen* and *Mademoiselle.*

Real life has few pat situations, no definitive solutions, and no happy endings. Elise begins the last chapter of her narrative with a tone of mild regret: "I wish I could end on that high note. But I see now that life never stays pitched on such high, triumphant, dramatic notes. Those moments come and are important and change everything, but they fade also, and reality, with its shifting hues, blurs everything."

9. Adult Fiction: "The Ingredients of Popular Success"

Norma Klein has not been especially pleased with the reception of her adult fiction. She feels that her very prominence in the young adult field has hindered her acceptance into the literary mainstream, beside such writers as Alice Adams, Anne Tyler, and Margaret Drabble, to name some of her favorites. In the *Publisher's Weekly* article where she describes herself as a "mid-list author" of adult fiction, she acknowledges that her books for adults will be published, will attract a limited readership, and will make some money.[1] The further implication would seem to be that they will be inadequately reviewed, will not receive full-page critiques in the *New York Times,* and will not be featured in *Ms.* or assigned in college classrooms. They will also not be purchased by Hollywood for film adaptation.

Though Klein, to make her point, sometimes exaggerates her neglect by the literary establishment—her work is more widely acknowledged than she sometimes feels in her more pessimistic moments—it must be conceded that her better adult books have not received the attention their quality merits.

Despite the well-known difficulties in the classification of Klein books, several of her novels are adult fiction by any reasonable definition. This fiction is, furthermore, of considerable quality. Klein certainly writes better than many authors who are much better known for "serious women's fiction," the genre concerned primarily with love, marriage, parenthood, and, more lately, career problems.

These novels about "the developmental tasks of adulthood" in most hands tend to be repetitive, whether written by Gail Godwin, Ellen Gilchrist, Alice Adams, or scores of others. Nora Ephron's *Heartburn* came out a bit better than most fiction in the "marriage and adultery" category because of the author's genuine wit. Klein's wit also serves her well. She is, in fact, one of the more skilled practitioners of this type of fiction, whose attitudes and values are unfortunately fast becoming clichés. If she does not escape the repetition that eventually makes this fiction tiring, then neither do her more acclaimed competitors.

A principle reason for Klein's relative neglect as a writer of adult fiction is that her best work has been in the short story form. While the short story or novelette may provide much artistic satisfaction and has been the preferred form of several masters who find their place in the canon taught in schools, its market in the United States today has almost evaporated. The professional who is financially reliant upon her work finds little encouragement to write short fiction. Klein's stories have appeared in some of the most prestigious and excellent "little magazines," but payment there is minimal and sometimes nonexistent. The journals that do pay well, such as the *New Yorker* and *Cosmopolitan,* find her tales, Klein believes, to be either too eccentric or too long. The elongated short story of forty pages or so, possibly Klein's most congenial form, continues to present this major marketing problem. Such a narrative would consume a good part of an entire issue of the *Sewanee Review,* for example, and yet would be too brief for a book. For financial reasons Klein has in recent years found it necessary to abandon this form, in which she truly excels, although she continues to write adult novels.

Among the published writings to date that are unequivocally designed for mature readers are six novels, of moderate interest to the general reader, and two short story anthologies, which are among the strongest of all Klein's writings and should take their place among distinguished American short story collections.

Give Me One Good Reason, published in 1973, is by far the most significant of the novels. The extensive self-analysis by the protagonist is frequently insightful. Gabrielle is a biochemical researcher, a single woman in her middle thirties who makes a calm decision to have a child. Though she lives in a liberal urban environment, New York City, in a reasonably permissive decade, and is financially comfortable, she soon is involved in enough complications to sustain a reader's interest throughout a substantial book. Gabrielle chooses the father of her child with some care. He is Matthew, the man she has been living with for five years. He is a French professor who is an authority on Baudelaire. Though he is willing to take some limited responsibility for the child, Matthew is a bisexual who has no desire for sustained family life. Gabrielle is not displeased and, anyway, insists that the baby be totally hers.

Her parents are among the first to be notified of her decision. Though her father is pleased at the prospect of having another grandchild, even under these circumstances, her mother's chief concern is that Matthew is not being duly considered, a point Gabrielle dismisses rather lightly. A more thorny problem is presented by her boss in the laboratory where she works, a prissy and unattractive Polish-American. Though she has expected him to be shocked by her impending motherhood, she has not anticipated his actual reaction when he learns she is pregnant: an offer of marriage, a quaint and grotesquely humorous gesture.

Though she is able to pacify her boss with reasonable excuses, Gabrielle finds that despite everything she is a bit embarrassed when she starts wearing her maternity clothes. On the whole, however, she savors her pregnancy and the eventual birth of her child. Even though she had hoped for a daughter, she is delighted with her son, a baby so ideal in behavior that Klein was initially criticized for making it all too easy on her fictional unmarried mother.

The narrative becomes less interesting and believable when

Gabrielle begins a romance with Rudolf, a taxi driver who befriends her on the New York streets and turns out to be a medical doctor between jobs. Rudolf soon leaves New York for the West Coast, where he is to work in, of all places, an abortion clinic. It is as if Klein felt it necessary, after asserting the right of a single woman to have a child, to make an equal time pitch for "pro-choice." Gabrielle's romance with Rudolf is also a little grotesque; she is, after all, a sort of madonna figure, a bringer of life, while he is a minister of fetal death. This touch of "black humor" was certainly intentional.

The critics who found that Gabrielle had it too easy were, at least in part, right. As an unmarried mother, she seems a bit too lucky. Everything goes her way: a superfluous lover who is the father of her child removes himself without protest, parents understand, and her job is not lost as a result of her social defiance. She even gains the supportive affection of another man who is a medical doctor. Though Klein is writing about one woman who has made a calm decision and is in a position to handle its consequences, several readers were not slow to point out that most single mothers, unlike Gabrielle, face a host of defeating problems. While Klein has the right to deal with an atypical situation, the tensions of her plot would have been keener had there been at least an acknowledgment that social attitudes are not purely capricious but are generally based on wisdom derived from years of community experience. In addition, the book does have a didactic tone, which opens it to social criticism. Pregnancy for the vast majority of single women—who are usually struggling against adversity and are all too frequently members of disadvantaged minority groups—is the greatest single source of permanent poverty. Reading *Give Me One Good Reason* might leave the unreflective reader with the impression that the general social disapproval of unmarried motherhood is no more than an archaic prejudice.

Coming to Life, published in 1974, is a story of adultery and marriage gone sour. Despite genuine elements of interest, the publisher was certainly extravagant in comparing this book to the novels of Kate Chopin and Doris Lessing. Though the market has now been saturated with similar novels, this is still one of the better "women's narratives," tackling the problem of middle-class wife abuse and promoting the idea that wives can liberate themselves from intolerable marriages through self-assertion and education. *Publisher's Weekly* was accurate in its critique of *Coming to Life:* "Although it has some of the elements of traditional 'women's fiction,' this is a good cut above much of that genre, both as an exploration and as a novel."[2]

If *Coming to Life* had been written by anyone other than an author of Jewish background, it might well have been denounced as anti-Semitic. With one exception, the Jewish characters in the book are thoroughly unpleasant. They are ill-talking personalities with profane, vulgar tastes, atypical Klein creations. They are, however, individuals rather than representative ethnic types, and Klein is correct when she observes that membership in a group provides a certain license to be critical in ways that would be offensive if coming from an outsider.

Girls Turn Wives appeared in 1976. It provides an intelligent exploration of sex roles and the influence of the women's movement on two married women, their husbands, their children, and their lovers. There is little that is unusual or startling in the book, other than a brief episode of child molestation that appears to have no lasting ill effects on anyone concerned and no strong repercussions.

Wives and Other Women (1982) may be a bit more skillful in its handling of some of the same themes as the previous two books and in its juggling of a ten-year time span. While this adult novel was an attempt at contemporaneity in its treatment of "open marriage," the sexual revolution, the feminist movement, and the problems of adjustment they all bring, it does not add much to Klein's previous treatment of the issues. Though the publisher's publicist claimed it to be "both funny and deeply moving," it does not measure up in either quality to Klein's best young adult fiction.

Lovers, which appeared in 1984 and is dedicated to Norma Klein's father, explores the lives of two couples, from their thirties into their fifties. Again the time frame is juggled with considerable expertise, with interesting if highly judgmental observations provided on the shifting mores of the period. This tale about a long-term adulterous affair is again moderately entertaining but lacks real focus and center. There is some mildly amusing discussion of Jewish-gentile and black-white marriages and interactions, and the commentary of the characters about the "ridiculousness" of the Jewish as well as other religions suggests an authorial intrusion that may or may not seem relevant to the reader.

American Dreams, the most recent adult novel, was published in 1987. Its plot follows the lives of four individuals, two women and two men, through two critical decades for American society. There is an aggressive feminist, an aspiring writer, an internationally known photographer, and a second male who—endowed with extraordinary good looks, talent, and affluence—would appear to be especially privileged. Actually, he is painfully torn between his closet homosexuality and his desire for a life society regards as normal. The careers of the four characters are neatly intertwined; the plot's architecture is perhaps the most intricate of all Klein's books. Though it is composed with the author's characteristic competence, *American Dreams* has little to distinguish it from scores of similar books. Once again, an assortment of men and women aspire to achieve their versions of the American dream. Yet there is no strong sense of the deeper meaning of the American events of the sixties and seventies, which supposedly shaped these characters and their aspirations. The reader is left with a sense of déjà vu. This story has been more grippingly told before, by other novelists and even by Klein herself. Like most of Klein's adult novels, *American Dreams* is readable but lacks the originality and compelling thrust of the young adult fiction.

There has been speculation from time to time about why Klein chooses to write so often of adultery, troubled marriages, and divorces when she herself came from a stable family and has been happily married to the same man for more than twenty years. Perhaps a Freudian analyst could provide tantalizing explanations, but two reasons immediately suggest themselves. Klein is a popular writer, who often chooses the subjects that she feels will interest her audience, such as marital problems and changing sexual mores. Furthermore, her concern with the complexities of intimate human relationships may be another tribute to her psychiatrist father. Klein treats the intricacies of people's personal problems, whether petty or serious, with the compassion and sophistication one would expect of a good therapist.

Klein is a good observer and, judging from her skill with dialogue, apparently a good listener. She admits to having learned much from listening to her friends speak of their lives and problems. Especially on visits to her husband's small hometown, she has mentally recorded her impressions, discovering material everywhere for her fiction. In writing about family and marital turmoil Klein is following the same traditions, mining the same vein, as other writers she admires, even though the characters and situations are fast becoming clichés. Yet the publicist for St. Martin's Press is no doubt excessively enthusiastic in observing on the dust jacket of *Wives and Other Women:* "If ever a book had the ingredients for popular success this is it!"

If it still rankles to be merely a "midlist" author of adult novels when one is a superstar in the young adult field, Klein might well take stock of her writings in the former category. While she has been original, daring, and innovative in the youth books, her adult novels seem a bit stale and repetitive. Nothing makes them distinctive in their genre. They are neither inept nor stylistically dazzling.

Notoriety in the popular fiction field is in part a matter of personality exploitation by the media. The Klein personality has not been widely advertised. Perhaps because she has never been the media celebrity that Judy Blume has become, Klein's adult fiction has not stirred the same curiosity that greeted a Blume adult novel of a few years ago. The very novelty of a mainstream novel by "the kids' favorite" attracted reviewers and readers to Blume's offering. Yet Klein's novels are distinctly more professional. Also, Norma Klein, one feels, would be a great success on television or the lecture circuit. She is highly articulate, lively, telegenic, and has interesting opinions and sometimes outrageous ways of expressing them. Most of all, she is very likable. No doubt media celebrity would generate interest in her largely unknown adult writings.

Klein's loyal teenage fans will grow up; they might be a potential readership for the adult fiction. Yet there is some indication that a youth audience, no matter how devoted, may experience subconscious resistance to hanging on to a favorite author from adolescence. In maturity there is a sense of "putting away childish things," rejecting the parent, which may even, however unfairly or counterproductively, include casting aside a storyteller cherished in youth.

While the adult novels, though competently constructed, quickly fade in memory, the same cannot be said for Klein's short stories. They are superb. Not only have they been placed in such prestigious quarterlies as the *Sewanee Review,* but they have been anthologized in *Prize Stories 1963: The O. Henry Awards, Prize Stories 1968: The O. Henry Awards,* and *The Best American Short Stories of 1969.* The short story is, in fact, not only a major strength of American fiction in general, it is an ideal form for Klein. She has especially enjoyed writing stories and yearns to produce more, if only marketing conditions were more favorable. As a short story writer, she is fully in command of the complexities of her craft. Like her master, Chekhov, she is able to inject a vast emotional range into tightly controlled stories narrated with seeming objectivity. Though her range of character types is considerably more limited than Chekhov's, within her own selected limits Klein is thoroughly at ease.

Two collections of outstanding short stories, *Love and Other Euphemisms* and *Sextet in A Minor,* were published in 1972 and 1983 respectively. The stories were published as a favor to the author, even though the publishers expected to earn little from their sales. The individual narratives had appeared originally in respected but mostly noncommercial journals. In these stories, consistently well-crafted and sometimes very strong indeed, Klein demonstrates her vast superiority to scores of short story writers who are better known. She is potentially one of America's masters of the form.

The stories in *Love and Other Euphemisms,* the first anthology, appeared from 1967 through 1972 in both mass circulation publications and little magazines: *Mademoiselle, Mad River Review, Prairie Schooner,* and *Cosmopolitan.* Artistically framed, thoughtful in thematic structure, and finely wrought, there is little in these narratives that is extraneous. The writing is always firmly controlled. "Pratfalls," a novelette of 154 pages, is perhaps the most interesting of the lot. It tells the story of Rachel, a woman of erratic personality from a poor Jewish background who marries a black professional from a wealthy family. Although there are hints that in Rachel's disordered way she may actually love her husband, she likes to believe she married him for less personal, purely idealistic reasons. She cannot bring herself to admit that she is actually a Cinderella who has landed a coveted husband with inherited wealth and the professional status of an astronomer. Instead of a black revolutionary, she has acquired a husband with the habits and attitudes that come from financial comfort and professional success.

Leaving her husband with an angry note protesting his inability to live up to her ideological expectations, Rachel moves into a small apartment with a French male homosexual. She also enrolls in a school for clowns and is soon in partnership with a lesbian friend providing entertainment at parties. In the meantime, she has the obligatory affair, this time with a wealthy white man. She conceives twins, though she is unsure whether by her husband or her lover. Despite their dubious paternity, the infants' arrival is eagerly awaited by all the interested parties. Rachel plans to name them Angela and Kathleen, in honor of black revolutionaries Angela Davis and Kathleen Cleaver. There is some suspense as she becomes precariously reconciled with her husband and they await the revelation of the twins' color. When the babies turn out to be black, everyone breathes a sigh of relief. Though she still has problems with her husband's lack of "negritude," Rachel returns to him. To everyone's intense embarrassment, she puts on black face and does a mammy act at a wedding reception held for another member of his family.

Though she professes great contempt for the rich, Rachel seems to attract only prosperous, successful men. She thinks of blacks and Jews as the world's two great outcasts, groups she champions. Though the exploits of her own chaotic family support her image of them as losers, the ordered lives of her husband's relatives suggest that they are among the world's winners, whatever their color. While she can never quite forgive her husband for not being "a woolly-haired dashiki-wearing revolutionary," she sinks, however apologetically, into the luxury he can provide. A pratfall is an indelicate fall on one's bottom; even though men always rescue her, Rachel carries an enormous chip on her shoulder, a constant sense of having the rug pulled out from under her. She sees herself as the archetypal loser. Her feelings are masterfully conveyed to the reader, even while Klein never quite captures the milieu of the black high bourgeoisie in which Rachel awkwardly moves.

In "Apocalypse at the Plaza," another fine story in the collection, an unstable man who calls himself an artist commits acts of minor aggression as the only way he can protest the oh-so-civilized postmatrimonial situation in which he finds himself. His former wife and her current husband try to extend him hospitality and even want to give him an air-conditioning system, with the inevitable condescension such generosity implies. Left alone in their hotel suite, the artist expresses his warped aesthetic and sexual impulses by cutting his former wife's fashionable and expensive dresses into interesting patterns.

"An American Marriage" is the tale of a marital breakup, where money, mutual hostility, and recriminations abound. Images of aging women in Florida in "varying stages of disintegration" and a middle-aged housewife in a flowered duster leaping from a six-story window to her death reinforce a despairing sense of desolation. Two therapists of different styles can do little to patch up the fading marriage. Carol, the wife, sees an expensive Viennese psychiatrist who looks like T. S. Eliot and whose enormous fees are paid without protest by her parents. Mike, her less affluent husband, goes to the Treatment Center in midtown Manhattan where he is counseled with equal ineffectiveness by an informal swinger type psychotherapist.

"The Boy in the Green Hat" is a haunting story with an air of mystery. Lang's wife tells him that a peculiar thing happened in the park. She and their son Avram were followed by a boy in a green hat. Lange is troubled because his wife has been mentally ill, and he has been warned to be alert for signs of a recurrence. Her pregnancy of three months presents an additional complication. After many inquiries, Lang manages to locate a boy in a green hat, alone in the park, dreamily watching the other children. When he returns home to tell his wife he too has seen the boy, she looks at him blankly and uncomprehendingly. Is he beginning to share her delusions? Which of them is insane?

"A Sense of Ritual" is a very good, characteristic Klein story about a modern wedding, which lacks sexual curiosity, the suspense of a lingering betrothal, and the sacramental blessing of religion. A couple who have been living together decide, after considerable hesitation, to be properly married. The bride feels she is compromising her principles by getting married in the first place. At one of the social festivities attending the wedding, she tries to shock the guests by wearing a bikini. She is even apologetic when she decides to visit her hairdresser before the ceremony.

Feeling a need for more than just the services of City Hall and a justice of the peace, the couple see the groom's old college chaplain. The clergyman does not mind that the bride—who has the unlikely name of Maggie Thatcher—is Jewish or that the groom, Dave, is Protestant. But he decides that since neither of them is religious he cannot in conscience give them his professional blessing. The chaplain, nevertheless, recommends a Unitarian minister who has fewer scruples. This second minister offers them a selection of services. They may have a "traditional service" in which they agree to cherish, to have and to hold, and where the name of God is invoked to look over the couple and preserve their happiness. Or they may choose a "semi-traditional service" in which they agree to similar things but with less frequent appeals to deity. A third option calls for vaguely humanistic platitudes to be uttered, totally without reference to any Divine Being. They choose the secular service but add traditional vows. As a further gesture toward tradition, they decide to abstain from sex for one night before their ceremony.

Klein admits that "A Sense of Ritual" was inspired by the circumstances of her own wedding, which sealed a loving, permanent commitment. Even without the ceremony that once attended marriage in traditional Jewish or Christian societies, the institution, this story seems to say, is still popular and most persons entering it intend it for life. Only after the wedding ceremony does Maggie achieve her moment of epiphany, realizing "that love was her sense of ritual," that love is more important than her former rebelliousness.

"Magic" is a less ambitious but still evocative story in which the death of actress Marilyn Monroe runs like a thread. Melissa, the protagonist, has been told that she looks a bit like Monroe. She also feels that, like Monroe, her real self and her public image are at variance. Her approaching marriage, she hopes, will aid in integrating her personality. Through a series of events, in which the problems of her future family-in-law are more fully revealed, Melissa comes to realize that she should probably not marry at this point in her life. The proposed marriage was an escape; she concludes that she can, unaided, accept herself more realistically. Marilyn Monroe, the lonely suicide unable to separate myth from reality, is seen as one who allowed herself to be trapped by a false image. She was not merely a victim of others but a victim of her own obsessions. Melissa resolves that she will not be spiritually murdered by such a false image.

The second anthology of stories, *Sextet in A Minor,* was published in 1983, again as a publisher's favor to a successful author whose other books were moneymakers. The stories that were collected originally appeared in *Quarry,* the *Southwest Review, Prairie Schooner,* the *University of Windsor Review,* the *University Review,* and the *Denver Quarterly.* The story "The Wrong Man," which appeared first in *Quartet,* was later reprinted in *Prize Stories 1974: The O. Henry Awards.*

Each narrative of the collection is interesting in its own often unusual way. The title story, another of those novelettes of which

Klein is especially fond, is an intricately plotted narrative of an encounter between six Americans in the Italian Alps. All six characters are woven in and out of focus in a remarkably skilled tapestry. "Easter Rabbit in July" is the tale of a double adultery, played out with interesting symbolism. A Jewish man, whose wife is having an affair with a rabbi, purchases on impulse a stuffed Easter rabbit with a small defect. On sale in July, it seems a good buy, though he realizes that others may find it strange that a Jewish male has concern for either a flawed rabbit or a flawed rabbi!

"Someone's Face at the Door" is the more poignant story of Edward, who takes his German girlfriend to the apartment of his former parents-in-law, a Jewish psychiatrist and his intense and elegant wife. The mission is to collect Edward's son, but first the haunting memory of Sylvia, the deceased wife, must be confronted. Sylvia was a poetic woman who used to play Beethoven on the piano. Then, seemingly without any reason, she threw herself from one of the windows of her apartment. Sylvia's parents cannot disguise their hostility to the German goy girlfriend, who seems likely to become Edward's second wife. To them she seems little more than another Nazi come to take what belongs to the Jews. Edward, who is a museum curator by profession, remembers that Sylvia had first attracted his attention because of her resemblance to a Botticelli maiden. It was her constant melancholy, which he had found so plaintively appealing at first, that had finally wrecked their marriage. And he blames her for having chosen such a gaudy way to die. Her parents know in their hearts that Edward could have done little to save their daughter. Despite their own wealth and psychological sophistication, they too had been unable to help her.

Edward's self-understanding is crucial to the narrative. When he compares his German girlfriend to his ex-wife, he believes that he has changed and matured as the result of his bitter experiences. Yet the reader perceives that he still reduces women to art; his wife-to-be, without the long flowing hair and vague, romantic eyes of the vanished Sylvia, is more like the curved and flushed women of the Dutch and Flemish masters.

"The Interview" introduces as protagonist Renata, an Italian journalist of the Oriana Fallaci mold. She interviews a movie star, talks with a film director, and meets her father for lunch, probing relentlessly into other people's personal lives, without coming to terms with her own restless, nervous existence. When she writes happy accounts of celebrity lives for American magazines Renata recognizes the falsity of it all. After the lunch with her father, she takes stock, acknowledging that she is caught in the dilemma of the liberated woman without a man. Her career has been motivated by the urgency of avoiding the fate of her mother, a woman emotionally and financially dependent upon a man who has affairs, a woman whose only recourse has been migraines, overeating, and tears. Renata herself has been able to travel, make money, meet interesting people, and avoid depression—all by writing articles so silly that she would never have read them had they been written by anyone else. "One avoids one trap and falls into another," she thinks as she goes her way.

"Patsy's Demise" is an interesting tour de force in which a woman's suicide is discussed by her "closest friend" and her ex-husband. Everything is related in dialogue, with considerable irony and satire. Suicide in this instance, the story seems to be saying, was an affirmation of life, a solid protest against the lives of quiet desperation that Thoreau said most people lead.

"The Gray Buick" is an especially intriguing story, in part because it is so unlike Klein's other writings. Although not much happens, except that a woman has a nightmare in a motel where she is trysting, there is a mood of Freudian horror or impending madness that is sustained throughout. The story begins much like an episode from "Alfred Hitchcock Presents" or even "The Twilight Zone." A gray Buick, which may or may not be driven by a ruffian sent by the woman's husband, appears to follow the lovers. In the woman's dream she believes she is being abducted. She also sees—whether in her dream or in reality is not clear—a honeymooning girl at another window of the motel. The girl is naked and has a strange smile.

Even the minor stories in the collection are provocative. In "Possessions," a curious role reversal is seen to have taken place when a lonely woman meets her former boss-lover again after ten years; in "Mementos," a repressed man's divorce, the sale of his house, and his Jewish self-hatred are deeply entangled; in "The Missed Sunday," a woman flirts disastrously with her former husband at his second wedding ceremony; in "The Cuckold," a content and well-adjusted gay man visits a heterosexual friend who is collapsing mentally. "Sleeping Pills" and "The Wrong Man" are stories of psychological exploration, repressed sexuality, and suicide; "The Chess Game" is a bitter account of a visit to a mental institution where a deranged father can still sadistically use a chess game to torment his son; and "The Babysitter" is a frightening account of a repressed, mentally ill woman who experiences life entirely through others and perversely acknowledges that she has found her perfect vocation as a family babysitter.

The collected short stories of Norma Klein are polished gems, carefully plotted and finished with much care. While some tales stand out from the others, there is not a failed story among them. The images and symbols are as carefully chosen as those of a skilled poet. Though her mood, atmosphere, preoccupations, and milieu are quite different from those of Chekhov, in these finely wrought stories Klein shows herself again a disciple of the master of the "well-made" story.

Most of the problems the critics complain of in Klein's young adult fiction—the looseness of construction, carelessness of detail, repetition, the sermonizing—are surmounted in the tales, so evocative and devoid of didacticism. What is important to these stories is the unfolding of a character, the relating of an incident, or the revelation of an insight, and not the pressing of a point or the defending of a thesis. The stories are genuine works of literary art, not merely lively narratives. It is perhaps incidental that, taken together, they also succeed where the adult novels sometimes fail: they make meaningful statements about the lives of women. The reviewer in *Nation* expressed the central vision effectively: "Written in prose that is lively, quick, and sure, these tales of the mismarried, of stolen but unenthusiastic adulteries, of marriages that frame shock treatments and suicide confirm yet again that if marriage and men are still remarkably much on women writers' minds, it is mostly as disordered thoughts and bad dreams."[3]

10. The "Outrageous" Norma Klein

No other writer of teenage fiction, not even the more widely read Judy Blume, has been as heatedly discussed by librarians, teachers, and concerned parents as has Norma Klein. While Klein's adult fiction passes as relatively tame for her era, the young adult writings have constantly elicited comment and sometimes outrage.

From her liberal urban perspective, Klein may occasionally be bewildered by the responses of provincial America to her books. Her juvenile novels use expletives rarely; they generally have tame, unimaginative titles and do not revel in the anatomical features of sexual acts. Klein has accurately noted that the constant evening fare on television is consistently more shocking than anything in her fiction. Yet Americans do exert a special protectiveness toward the printed word. Television and films are regarded as ephemeral. Eddie Murphy's four-letter expletives pass in movies without much notice. Yet print arouses concern because it seems—at least to those who do not understand how books are here yesterday, remaindered today, and gone tomorrow—immutable.

Klein's further defense might be that she is simply writing about what young adults are saying and doing. Drugs, sexual experimentation, and family crises are a part of the scene. To ignore them when writing about teenagers is to falsify experience.

In actual fact, since Klein writes chiefly about the upper middle class, her narratives are considerably tamer than those of her more gritty colleagues in the field, such as Rosa Guy, Walter Dean Myers, and Harry Mazer.

Despite Klein's convincing justification for her practices, the reader cannot totally escape the suspicion that in part she actually delights in shocking and relishes her notoriety. When she ventures to Washington state or Georgia to defend one of her books against a public outcry, she seems to savor the role of bold champion of both individual and artistic freedom. There is no question that she is an articulate and entertaining spokeswoman for her point of view.

Klein attempted to explain herself in the 1979 edition of *Contemporary Authors:* "What draws me most [to the juvenile and young adult fiction categories] is that I feel the children's book field has been and is still weighed down by taboos on many subjects, on abortion, sex, the human body, etc. I feel one could write a book a year till one was just touching on each of these taboos. . . . We need books where children masturbate, think about their parents' sex lives, enjoy the physical sensations provided by their bodies. We need books that are non-punitive, open, honest. There aren't enough, not nearly."[1]

With her manifesto on record, however overstated for effect, it is fair to explore Klein's motivations and evaluate her success in educating her public to accept the books she feels young people deserve.

There are a number of reasons why authors may wish to shock. Some wish to be titillating, sensational, and much discussed in order to make money and attract attention to themselves. Other writers have more serious social and aesthetic motivations. They may wish to shock their readers out of complacency, sounding an alert to a problem that needs understanding and attention. They may wish, like certain famous writers of the past, to start a crusade through fiction. Why not free the American slaves, or the Russian serfs, or reform the meat-packing industry? They may feel an urgency to proclaim a crisis view of life, a grim philosophical or religious stance. A writer may even strive to achieve a dark aesthetic, as, for example, in absurdist drama or the theater of cruelty. Or the motive may be, less ambitiously, merely to avoid sentimentality, eliminate platitudes and cant, and come to grips in fiction with genuine existence.

Norma Klein's motives in defying the social conventions of young adult fiction are no doubt as intricate and ambiguous as the motives of any complex, intelligent individual generally are. She probably does enjoy the attention she receives for being the boldest of juvenile writers at the same time that she frequently finds the attacks on her work wearisome. If so, she is certainly not the first writer to savor contradictory sentiments.

But Klein is a serious artist, even a crusader, as well as a commercial writer. She does desire to liberate her audience from what she perceives as limiting attitudes and conduct. She wishes to free her readers from inhibitions that she believes prevent the rich exploration of life. She also wants to show that indeed not all children live in the two-parent households that have been so idealized by earlier fiction. Mothers are not negligent because they must work. Fathers must even sometimes rear children, and frequently they do a superb job of it. Not all single parents take vows of celibacy. Some mothers, in fact, may choose girlfriends rather than boyfriends, and yet they may still be capable, successful parents.

Klein likes to overturn the clichés, reversing expectations. Teenage pregnancy is no longer the fear that paralyzes high-school sexual activity. Mothers—and even fathers—can dispense diaphragms. If this fails, abortion is available, and no one need feel guilt over it, though even in Klein fiction one frequently does. Options are many. Blacks and whites may sleep together, marry, and produce well-adjusted children. Sex roles are no longer rigidly defined. A woman may be a doctor, or she may be a fashion model. A boy may be a cheerleader. Opportunities open in all directions. Even Jewish boys do not always have to become doctors, measuring up to their parents' ideas of achievement. They may be artists or operate used-car lots.

It is probably to the credit of Klein, Judy Blume, and a few other serious yet bold writers that subjects that appeared shocking in the teenage novel only six or seven years ago are now generally acceptable. Youth fiction is, of course, following a trend in the total culture toward more openness. Yet Klein's loyal readers know that the last thing this particular author wants to do is become part of a comfortable establishment. Her thirst for honesty is as strong as ever, leading her even more deeply into areas that continue to trouble adults whose critique of teenage books rarely goes beyond the moralistic.

It is instructive to review the chief taboos Klein has tackled in her fiction and to examine more closely her manner of attack. It is also worthwhile to identify several areas still regarded as indelicate into which she has ventured only by implication or not yet at all.

Klein is far from alone among important contemporary young adult writers in examining mental disturbance, drugs, and death. Only their ignorance of the field leads some adult readers to believe this fiction is still obsessed with sports, dating, and minor readjustments of relationships with parents. In *Hiding* and *Older Men,* Klein dealt with the subject of mental illness but suggested hope for its sufferers. Drug use figures less prominently in her writing than in that of several other proponents of young adult neo-realism. Families may occasionally use drugs recreationally, but no lasting harm is done. Klein's privileged urbanites are protected from the problems of the barrios, ghettos, and the city streets. No rescue missions or derelict shelters are needed for them; a good Park Avenue psychiatrist will suffice.

Of all Klein's characters, Jason in *Angel Face* comes closest to having a drug problem. The reader, who likes him, understands his need for a crutch, since school is so distasteful and his family is disintegrating. Though he spends a good part of each school week "spaced out," he does not seem headed toward disaster. He may even have discovered a crude adolescent way of coping with an otherwise impossible situation by escaping into a mild drug use. Indeed, he shows suprising maturity and composure at the sudden, suicidal death of his mother. Yet he pays a price. He will certainly not get into one of those fine eastern colleges that are such obsessions with Klein characters. If his drug stupor had not intensified his self-absorption, he might even have forestalled his mother's suicide. Though he will have to live with this knowledge for the rest of his life, he is obviously not irreparably damaged. The reader knows that with the support of his father, stepmother, and sympathetic older sister, he will survive this crisis too.

In Victorian and Edwardian books, righteous young people frequently died, bloodlessly and beautifully. Whatever Klein's professed existentialist view of the human experience, it seems clear that her fiction is more in the comic than in the tragic mode. Her narratives continue to end more frequently in marriages than in deaths. She has not, however, totally ignored death in her books. *Angel Face* in particular demonstrated considerable courage in its treatment of the mother's suicide, and *Going Backwards* has moved a long way toward freeing Klein fiction from superficial optimism.

Religion has been an even greater taboo in juvenile writing than sex and death. While the federal courts have decreed that "benevolent neutrality" is the proper attitude of the public schools toward the subject, teachers, librarians, and school boards have usually handled the matter more gingerly. Publishers of books for youth in the mass audience have often attempted to ignore religion. A foreign observer of the American popular media might never know that the United States is one of the most actively religious countries in the world. When children's books have in recent years started mentioning religion, their authors have been praised as courageous, even when the treatment has been glib and superficial, as in Judy Blume's *Are You There God? It's Me, Margaret* or M. E. Kerr's *Is That You, Miss Blue?*

In interviews and on questionnaires Norma Klein continues to state that she has no religion. If pressed she reiterates her opinion that all religions are sexist and harmful. Some of her critics have felt that she lacks even an elementary awareness of religion as a sociological phenomenon and that the absence of religious practice or a sense of religious issues contributes to a certain flatness in her books.

Yet Klein has used the absence of religious belief, if not belief itself, effectively in a few of her books. While nobody would suggest that she possesses the spiritual pensiveness that gives such resonance to the fiction of Saul Bellow, Bernard Malamud, Isaac Bashevis Singer, or even, on occasion, Philip Roth, she has captured the wistfulness felt from time to time by those who no longer have faith.

"A Sense of Ritual," the short story Klein admits was based on her feelings at the time of her marriage, shows a young couple without religious belief still demanding some ceremony when they marry and calling in a Unitarian minister as the most nearly innocuous member of the clergy they can find to witness traditional vows made without appeal to the name of God.

An even more poignant example of religious rustlings, this time among teenagers, is found in *Snapshots*. Sean prepares for his bar mitzvah, though his thoroughly secular family must quickly join a synagogue so that he will have a place for the ceremony. He conscientiously learns Hebrew and studies Jewish tradition. Though he cannot articulate his reasons for wanting to be a part of the religious community his parents have rejected, and he is not even sure he believes in God, he knows that his bar mitzvah will be one of the most significant occasions of his life and that his Jewishness is an essential part of his self-discovery.

In *Sunshine* one of Klein's truly fine fictional moments occurs in the marriage ceremony of the dying heroine and her musician companion. Confined to her hospital bed, Kate is led through the ancient Jewish vows by a rock musician friend who once studied for the rabbinate. Though she and her new husband are not themselves Jewish and the ceremony carries no weight in Jewish law, they follow tradition by breaking the goblet, remembering even in their brief moment of bittersweet happiness the ancient destruction of the Jerusalem Temple and the sufferings of the people of Israel.

Regional prejudice, unlike racism, sexism, and religious bigotry, is frequently expressed without apology by sophisticated people. Probably no feature of Klein's work has caused more resentment outside her home base than her New York ethos. Though Klein could not reasonably be faulted for writing about the locale and people she knows, readers in Nashville or Birmingham, for example, may be reminded of the *New Yorker* cartoon map of the United States. New York City is America, even the center of the world, bordered on one side by the rest of the country, which is depicted as a wasteland, and on the other by China (Europe has somehow vanished). New York is the citadel of culture, of entertainment, of adventure. In the comfortable brownstones where they live in upper middle-class comfort, Klein's characters are well protected from the darker side of life in the metropolis. They do not get mugged or raped, and they are not approached by prostitutes and pimps in the streets.

To her credit, Klein does have the grace to sometimes satirize the snobbish New York attitudes that so many of her characters share. In *It's OK If You Don't Love Me,* the conflict between the values of the liberated New Yorker, Jody, and those of the strait-laced midwesterner, Lyle, are well developed and generate some of the best conversation and most amusing episodes of the book, considerably more interesting than the scenes where the couple explore one another's anatomies.

Though strong assertions of feminism are no longer a novelty in juvenile and young adult books and only cause consternation among isolated ideological groups, Klein has occasionally been accused of unnecessary abrasiveness in promoting the goals of the woman's movement. She has indeed constantly promoted feminism in her writing, occasionally at the expense of literary considerations. Beginning with her juvenile books, she has been outspoken in her desire to get rid of limiting sex role expectations, and she has sometimes approached this task with a wit lacking in most other writers with a cause. If in her young adult fiction Klein has promoted feminism with a fervor that some readers have found overly didactic, she has at the same time demonstrated the social and family dislocations resulting from the changing role expectations and the dissatisfactions engendered by the women's movement. Feminism has given the characters in Klein's books courage to maintain the unorthodox households that have sometimes disturbed the purchasers and distributors—not to mention the publishers—of her books. Unmarried mothers may be one thing in real life and may be acceptable in adult fiction, but the happy single mother in *Mom, the Wolf Man and Me* was an innovation in youth fiction. With her teen novel *Breaking Up* Klein came out squarely for freedom of sexual activity and orientation.

It is well-known that a book may be highly moral, even conventional, in its overall direction yet become the target of the bookburners because of its use of a four-letter word here and there, no matter how appropriate or realistic the context. (*The Catcher in the Rye,* a work of genuine art and compassion, is a classic example.) Let it never be said that Norma Klein shies away from four-letter words, though obviously she does not use them merely to be offensive. Occasionally four-letter words do realistically enter the vocabulary of her characters, yet, if anything, her young adults are less profane than their real-life counterparts. A Klein heroine has been known to reflect on the vocabulary most people use in describing lovemaking and reject the prevailing euphemisms, which slur the dignity of the act, yet object equally to the four-letter words all too often used in offensive contexts that have nothing to do with tenderness or love.

It is this occasional use of language still considered improper that, more than any other feature of her writing, has caused Klein censorship problems. Now she says that it probably was not worth insisting that these words remain. It would have been so much easier to have removed them, providing effective substitutions in order for the books to go on their way unfettered.[2] But it is certainly their chatter about penises and vaginas that makes Klein's young children in books such as *Naomi in the Middle* distinctive and realistic.

Although Klein has dealt with a number of delicate subjects in her young adult fiction, the bold treatment of teenage sexuality is definitely her forte. For her heroines and heroes, the first sexual experience is not merely a coming-of-age rite, it is a claiming of rightful inheritance. Protective parents are ready to cushion this transition into adulthood and provide contraceptives for their daughters. If an accident occurs, there is always the possibility of abortion. If an affectionate partner is not available, there is the much less satisfactory substitute of masturbation. Fidelity to the loving partner is desirable, though not absolutely essential, and a temporary change of partner should not always be regarded as a betrayal.

It goes without saying that the appearance in young adult books of unpunished sexual relationships outside of marriage, whether or not a realistic reflection of what is actually happening, continues to disturb many adults. It is not so much Klein's mere description of sexual activity that has troubled her critics, but her strongly implied approval of it.

Sexual adventures have greatly accelerated in some of Klein's more recent young adult novels. In earlier books, there was more buildup to the eventual sexual consummation. Now sex in the teen books has become almost as commonplace and casual as it is in adult novels by Klein and others. Young people change partners without much guilt or remorse. The change may even be presented to the reader, within the context of the narrative, as a mark of the character's greater maturity. He or she has grown up and moved on.

The increased tolerance of teenage sex both in society and in fiction does not, of course, mean that there is widespread approval of all the forms it may take. While Klein must now work harder to startle her readers, to find lingering taboos to violate, there are still a number of forbidden relationships to explore. And she *is* beginning to explore them.

Normal schools used to warn beginning teachers of that first rule of faculty-student behavior: no dates with students. In *Love is One of the Choices* Klein's characters violate this law with inpunity and add the further offense of adultery. The central relationship of the novel is atypical, because Klein's teenagers rarely have sex with older or married people (*French Postcards* was, after all, an adaptation of someone else's story). The emotional and psychological tensions so frequently generated in the classic French or Italian coming-of-age novel by the youth who experiences his initial sexual encounter with a sympathetic older adult has been lacking in Klein's work, as in most of American fiction. Caroline, the central character, not only sleeps with her high school science teacher while his mentally disturbed wife is away from home, but even ends up marrying him after his wife's suicide.

Interracial sex and marriage is another subject that even Klein admits is so "fraught" that she may not treat it again.[3] While black-white unions are now widely accepted, particularly in the more educated classes, there is still considerable hesitancy to introduce them into juvenile fiction. In *Angel Face,* Otis, the black youth, has an affair with a pretty Italian immigrant in his high school class, even though her Mafia-style older brothers, all too stereotypically, lurk threateningly nearby. Yet it is *Bizou* that presents—not wholly effectively—Klein's loudest statement of interracial sex and marriage.

Sex among the elderly is perhaps as bold a topic as any to introduce in the teenage novel, since young people otherwise accepting of the sexual styles of others may be offended by the overt sexuality of persons over forty, especially parents or—horrors!—grandparents. Yet Klein has provided an assortment of amorous senior citizens in her writing for young people.

In maintaining her schedule of attacking one taboo a year in the young adult field, it has not been necessary for Klein to even try to catch up with the daring of adult fiction. As we have seen, when she writes for adults, Klein elicits no startled responses. The conversations and situations of the young adult stories appear shocking only because the public is less accustomed to such frankness in this fictional category. In children's books little girls are not supposed to speculate openly about their parents' sexuality or the anatomy of their brothers, though everyone knows that in real life they do. When the young adult novel first became popular a few decades ago, heroines agonized over a goodnight kiss, as indeed their real human models did well into the 1950s. Now in both real life and in Klein fiction, a seduction often takes less time to plot than that famous kiss of the fifties. How nostalgic Maureen Daly's *Seventeenth Summer* now seems! Yet when teenage sexual activity appears in books designed for young people themselves, this clear finality of witness, of actually seeing it in print, is still perturbing to many adults.

Klein, it must be fairly acknowledged, is identifying undeniable features of American life. It is this life rather than the fiction reflecting it that really disturbs her critics. Klein is also fighting the battle against those who believe that the grit of real life is not an appropriate subject for young adult and children's literature, which should be edifying, that its raison d'être is to be didactic. Yet, at the same time, it is clear that Klein herself does not escape didacticism. In her sometimes overly intrusive lessons and in her stated credo that books should help liberate from social restraints, she is far from advocating art for art's sake.

Though she avoids the more obvious didacticism of juvenile fiction of earlier periods, Klein appears upon closer examination to lie within the established traditions of moralistic and therapeutic writing for youth. She is a sort of Miss Manners of fiction, with a high quality of wit and cleverness, addressing the questions and problems of her affluent young adult audiences, telling her readers to enjoy themselves—within reasonable limits—and reassuring them that life can be pleasant.

In recent years a few pundits have called for juvenile and young adult fiction that resembles the contribution of Émile Zola to mainstream French fiction in the late nineteenth century. Zola sought to depict the underside of French society, hoping his readers would become socially aware and would eventually use their influence to improve the plight of the poor and the maimed in body and mind. As early as 1970, Julius Lester demanded an American adolescent literature with "ghettos, slums, wars, and drunks lying on sidewalks" as the only way to train young people to deal with their social environment and to prevent them from becoming "emotional and spiritual amputees."[4] Others have proclaimed even more ardently that only fiction that reaches into the deep crevices of the inner city, revealing teenagers shooting drugs, fatally stabbing one another on subways, engaging in gang warfare, and being victimized by incestuous parents, deserves respectful attention. Only by dragging complacent young middle-class readers screaming through the hell of modern urban life, we are told, can youth be awakened to action that will eventually correct the conditions that stunt and destroy many children and adolescents. Again, such approaches to literature assume, as surely as did the writers of Victorian children's books, that literature exists to provide moral instruction or beneficial social consequences.

Norma Klein has not been a part of this Zolaesque mission to American youth. Possibly she lacks interest in the extremes of failure and poverty; she admittedly lacks experience in these areas. She has even implied that she regards the environment of her books as personal territory and that she does not want it inhabited by personalities too repugnant. Certainly no central Klein character has yet been found mugging passersby on the streets of New York to support a drug habit. The more recent novels have indeed started suggesting, however faintly, that there is another side to the city than its cultural and social glories, that outside the affluent apartment houses where most of the characters live lurks another world of crime and its devastated victims. Yet Klein characters are still cushioned from this world.

Naturalistic writers, following Zola's school, have often stressed sexuality as a disrupting drive, beyond human control. Klein's characters are indeed sexy individuals, driven—as are most real-life teenagers—by sexual impulses often dimly understood and sometimes ill-controlled. Yet Klein characters remain remarkably spared the consequences of any abuses of their sexuality. There are no women of the streets like Zola's Nana or Stephen Crane's Maggie; there is not even a Sister Carrie outlined in Dreiserian detail. The young mother in *The Swap* does have her life temporarily disrupted by an unplanned pregnancy and by her family's attitudes toward it, but she is later able to dispose of her child and her marriage easily, possibly wiser for the experiences. Klein views the expression of sexuality as basically healthy, more conducive to happiness than to sorrow, and problematic only when too many restrictions or unhealthy guilt surround it. Young people are asked to give remarkably little reckoning of their sexual adventures. If mistakes occur, protective parents move in to rectify them. These are the implied statements that Klein's more serious critics find oversimplifying.

Marriages frequently collapse in Klein's young adult novels, but her sometimes-too-obtrusive authorial voice is there to reassure the reader that a divorce does not necessarily mean that a marriage was a failure. A family of appealing children may exist to witness by their presence that good came from the dissolving union, and there is often a new mate—sometimes one for each of the parents—lurking in the wings to replace the discarded one. The new companion may appear more suitable for the next stage in the parent's character development. It is, however, probable that the general optimism of Klein's conclusions in her earlier young adult books was determined at least in part by the demands of her editors. *Older Men* and *Going Backwards* suggest that her work will probably develop in strength as she continues to defy editorial demands for Hollywood endings.

Klein genuinely likes almost every character she has created, and she rarely treats one badly. When asked why she has no villains and relatively few obnoxious characters, she usually suggests that her charitable attitude toward people is one result of the relatively sheltered life she has led. Working alone, largely her own boss, she has escaped the insults of the office and the frustrations of the marketplace that most working women have to face. The people she has known have been largely those of her choice; consequently, they have been pleasant and congenial. Whatever the explanation, as a realistic writer attempting to view life clearly and describe it without camouflage or euphemism, Klein may suffer from the liberal intellectual's characteristic deficiency of a sense of evil, whether personal or social. So often accused of being naughty-minded, Klein has actually erred in the other direction, failing to perceive many of the genuine abominations of contemporary life.

In *Bizou* the problem of child abandonment is treated superficially, though the desertion in that book is temporary and provisions, however inadequate, are made for the child during her mother's absence. *Domestic Arrangements* and *Older Men* flirt with family incestuous feelings, one of the last taboos in the novel of middle-class youth. While the leading characters in *Snapshots* were accused of pedophilia, they are clearly innocent even of the knowledge that such an offense exists. When homosexuals have been introduced in Klein novels, they have been consistently admirable and attractive individuals. The darker side of some gay lifestyles, the disease-ridden bathhouses and the criminals who prey on obsessively promiscuous homosexuals, have not appeared. Rape and violence are not a feature of Klein novels; nor does hellish, incurable mental disease afflict any of the young characters, though borderline psychosis and senility are portrayed. The brutalizing effects of poverty, not too visible from those Park Avenue apartments where Klein's characters live, are also not explored. Physical handicaps are presented in very positive ways in Klein's fiction, and will be further treated in books soon to be published; the message is that handicaps need not seriously interfere with active, joyful lives. While this is undeniably a good message for young adult books to bring, the grim devastation of some handicaps is real and has not been shown in Klein's books.

Despite the flutter that has surrounded the publication of several of her books, Klein is not even in the running for the title of "queen of teen-porn," as she has sometimes been flippantly labeled. Her writing is never salacious. At their best, her sex scenes are humorous and deeply revealing of character; at their worst, they are repetitive and flat. Despite several unorthodox sexual and family styles in her narratives, Klein's preference is definitely and even conventionally in favor of marriage, which she frequently bestows on her characters.

So it must be acknowledged: Norma Klein's books for young people are relatively genteel. Just as Henry James was called "the realist of the tea table" or "the naturalist in white kid gloves," Klein could be designated the neo-realist of affluence. She has frequently affirmed her desire to be upbeat and nonhurtful in her writings, to dramatize problems with the saving grace of humor. She has succeeded in this much more than in her desire to violate a taboo a year. Her books provide a relatively realistic glimpse of the lives of young people in a privileged class of American society. Though she lacks the elegiac quality that makes the adolescent stories of Philip Roth or, earlier, of Françoise Sagan so memorable, Klein is a talented miniaturist. She is at the same time an expanding writer, still youthful in outlook, sympathy, and curiosity; she writes well of characters in the limited milieu she has personally known, yet she shows evidence of talents more wideranging than thus far demonstrated. It is significant that her two most recent young adult novels, *Going Backwards* and *Older Men* are among her most courageous writings. She continues to grow. Her writing has been defiant but never really outrageous. The graduate of an elite college, Klein is a well-brought-up New Yorker who, despite the controversy that has surrounded some of her books, remains a fairly traditional housewife and mother. When her limited shock value dissipates and her critics stop twittering, she may be fully acknowledged as the skilled and still-developing writer she is. It seems likely that the most important Klein books are still to be written and it is almost certain that she will continue to be a major influence in young adult fiction.

Novels of the twentieth century, especially since the popularization of Freudian ideas, have frequently attempted penetrating psychological analyses of character. An entire school of literary criticism has developed to evaluate the success of this endeavor. Psychological insight is a properly recognized strength of Norma Klein. Quite possibly she has no superior in the entire field of young adult fiction when it comes to the understanding of subconscious forces that motivate human actions. All characters in Klein's writing, adults and children alike, are in part controlled by subconscious forces, which they but dimly if at all perceive. The protagonists persist in "acting out" and rationalizing impulses; sometimes their actions are better understood by others than by themselves. Will and rational choice do not always figure prominently. The resolution of impulses comes with "working them through" in the psychoanalytic sense. People get better to some degree on the basis of catharsis, but not always through real problem solving.

On the other hand, people in a Klein book frequently (but not always) are passive before fate; neither moral bravery nor villainy is really acknowledged. The narratives are populated by "nice" people, but rarely by heroically admirable individuals and never by genuine evildoers. Nor is there much stress on ideological or social forces; most of the action is the result of "private" impulses.

Thus Klein implies that there is a determinism exerted by the unconscious, with moral choices frequently governed by imperfectly comprehended impulses. Jane Austen, a writer much admired by Klein, implied a similar psychology in her fiction, while Dostoevsky, a writer Klein studied in school but does not find congenial, is diametrically opposite, with his stress on free will and the consequent full responsibility of each individual for his or her actions.

It is not difficult to understand why teenagers identify with Klein's fictional characters. A teenager usually feels heavily beset by problems. One of this author's enduring lessons for the young reader is that "you are not alone in having this feeling—everybody is 'screwed up' in his or her own way, and this applies even to people supposedly in authority, namely adults, sometimes especially to them." In a Klein book, the protagonist can best hope to "work it out" in the course of the narrative. This is rather like the conclusion of successful psychotherapy, which is believed to succeed when repressed emotions are brought to the surface and understood, a process having little to do with rational choice. So there is a conservative element of *acceptance* found in these books. Ethical concern is expressed by "working through" and not by any conscious acknowledgment of error. This type of resolution to conflict is most appropriate for teenagers, who wonder about all facets of adult life and yet feel they have little power over what happens in that world. Certainly one secret of Klein's great success in speaking to teenagers is this: whether on a rational level or intuitively, she understands their problems and feelings about the world and their own lives.

The unspoken tensions between the first-person narrator of each young adult book and the author herself, whose viewpoint is conveyed in each narrative, lead to a certain passiveness of plotting in the books, a watering-down of resolutions. Character is more important than external cause in establishing what happens. In fact, there are a limited number of external "causal" events—the feature that reviewers of Klein books frequently label "static"—which emphasizes the internal, drifting nature of the motivations of the characters. The protagonist and others drift to different "stages"—they move to California, go away to school, go to live with another parent, and so on, with each uprooting symbolizing the way the world is perceived by a teenager, who sees change coming but often without any clear "cause." A strength and a weakness in Klein's young adult books is the ruling out of moral concerns beyond psychological forces. The books ultimately express a deterministic philosophy in their failure to grant characters the full possibility of will and conscious resolution.

Klein, who is no stylistic innovator, would probably regard as pretentious writers who introduce into young adult fiction experimental techniques from impressionism or expressionism. Style in Klein's work, while never dazzling, is well suited to the point of view and intent of the books. The uncertainties of the young are captured in the flow of narrative—hesitant, sometimes broken, always revealing—in a way that is just short of brilliant. Stylistic flourishes would be inappropriate to both the narrators of these tales and the experiences they relate. While other contemporary writers of young adult narratives may appear to be more stylistically polished than Klein, this appearance is deceptive. Few have achieved her mastery of style as realized content, style that is so suited to the first-person narrators and thematic statements of each book that it is unobtrusive and, therefore, usually goes unnoticed.

While it is customary for favorable reviewers of Klein's books to mention in passing their "wit and wisdom," no one has previously proposed that Klein is a major humorist in young adult fiction. Yet she possesses in large measure one of the most coveted of all writing skills, the ability to make people laugh. Basically, her humor is achieved by creating genuinely funny characters, by placing them in odd or paradoxical situations, and by giving them unintentionally ironic and funny things to say. The comical features abound in every juvenile and young adult book she has written, perhaps with special effectiveness in those narratives that wrestle with involved problems and painful situations.

Though laughter-provoking characters appear in all the juvenile and young adult books, Klein's special gift of humor may be seen with particular force in the recent books that have a teenage male protagonist. This young hero, discovering girls, exploring life, and confronting crises, may be classified as a lovable schlemiel, a new embodiment of an old type from East European Yiddish fiction, celebrated in the tales of Sholem Aleichem, Isaac Loeb Peretz, and Isaac Bashevis Singer, and Americanized by Bernard Malamud, Philip Roth, and others. He is the archetypal loser, for whom destiny seems to bear a grudge, yet whose mishaps are usually funny rather than tragic. He is the pathetic clown, whose trials elicit laughter, even if through tears. Since teenagers, awkwardly caught between childhood and adulthood, always regard themselves as losers, it is not surprising that they pronounce as horrid many of the events that older people find funny. Encouragingly, Klein's young schlemiels consistently move beyond the "fall guy" stage during the course of their narratives. Prime examples of this amusing type are Jason in *Angel Face,* Sean in *Snapshots,* and Charles, the self-acknowledged loser of the Goldberg family, in *Going Backwards.*

Klein characters frequently find themselves in funny and ironic situations. Their very occupations and pastimes may make them the objects of laughter. Spence in *Give and Take* has a summer job as donor in a sperm bank. The bride in *Beginner's Love* is a funeral director. Sean in *Snapshots* is conscientiously preparing for his bar mitzvah when he finds himself under suspicion as a child pornographer. In *The Cheerleader* Evan and his Arab friend Karim become male cheerleaders in high fashion uniforms, put together by Karim's designer mother.

Klein's family scenes can also be very funny. Sometimes they are tinged with "black humor," long a mark of East European Yiddish fiction. The Thanksgiving dinner in *Angel Face* during which the mother announces her impending divorce from father— the dinner that gets totally out of control—is one example. In *Mom, the Wolf Man and Me,* Brett's friend, a little girl who lives with her divorced mother, is so obsessed with acquiring a father that she imagines the Tin Man in *The Wizard of Oz* as her dad. In *Going Backwards* there is even grim humor in the ramblings of the grandmother suffering from Alzheimer's disease.

Finally, there is the dialogue of Klein's characters, full of the nuances of life and the accents of urban speech. Klein has an excellent ear for speech rhythms. Dialogue in the juvenile books contains both the boldly funny strokes that children enjoy and the more subtle double entendres perceived by the adults who read these books to children. Almost any chapter of Klein's young adult books provides examples of lively speech made funny through the interactions of character, situation, and environment. *Mom, the Wolf Man and Me* offers a good illustration from a middle-level book. Brett is trying to explain to the children at school, who are celebrating Father's Day, that her mother is not married and is not divorced. She tells them that Mother has never had a husband. When they reply that it is impossible for mothers to have children all by themselves, that it takes male and female to make a baby, except perhaps with birds, Brett replies, in reference to her biological parents: "All I said was, they didn't get married . . . I didn't say she sat on an egg."

Klein's characters even have very funny interior monologues. In *Going Backwards* Charles is thinking about the sex life of his parents, with the distaste most young people feel in contemplating sexuality among their elders, especially their relatives. He reflects: "I've seen both of my parents naked and it decidedly was not a thrill. They're both in horrible shape. The thought of them engaging in any act requiring close physical proximity is repugnant to me. I hope they do it in the dark."

Hundreds of examples of Klein's humor could be easily presented. Her scenes are often so funny that a reader may burst into audible laughter while reading them silently. Because other features of her work have received so much attention, the fact that Klein is a humorist with few peers in the young adult field seems largely to have escaped the attention of her interpreters.

Norma Klein continues to publish books every year, and her readers seem guaranteed a generous supply for a long time to come. It would be indeed surprising to find such a prolific writer turning out masterpiece after masterpiece, year in and year out, yet her strengths have always outweighed her shortcomings. One may easily take issue with her sometimes casual treatment of sex, her occasional carelessness in detail, and her strong pronouncements, yet her books may be commended for avoiding the blandness—the desire to please as many groups as possible—that is sometimes found in juvenile and young adult books. If she has occasionally relied on some of the clichés of the young adult genre, she has, to her credit, added something unique to each book she has written.

In theme and plot it might be argued that she is the most courageous of young adult authors. She does not rest on her laurels, but continues through her contributions each year to expand the range of material acceptable in fiction for young people. Obviously undamaged by controversy, she is ready to stand up to editors and the public in order to express a conviction strongly held. She is a constant promoter of quality literature for young people, gaining more serious respect for the field by her efforts. Her range is much larger than generally recognized; when she moves beyond her established areas of strength, she is usually successful. She has a genuine comic talent, but can also be compassionate when she writes of serious situations and persons in crisis. Her ear for spoken language is frequently impeccable. Believable dialogue, which characterizes the individuals who speak it and, at the same time, advances the plot, has become a Klein hallmark.

Klein's books reveal a talented writer in command of her craft. The best of them are entertaining narratives for good readers of any age; in this regard, they pass the real test of merit for a book in any category. Furthermore, the young adult books are significant social documents, mirroring the preoccupations of their time: the sexual revolution of the sixties and seventies, feminism, the drug culture, and the interactions, from time to time, between generations, regions, and ethnic groups. Klein should not only be read for pleasure. Because of her vast influence on teenagers and her keen psychological insight, she should be studied by parents, teachers, counselors, and all others who work with the young.

Notes and References

Chapter 1

1. The statements of Norma Klein and information about her life and career come from personal correspondence; the Allene Stuart Phy interview with her in Lilburn, Georgia, 11 April 1986; the Mark West interview in New York City, 11 June 1985; and *Something about the Author,* Autobiography Series, ed. Adele Sarkissian (Detroit: Gale Research Co., 1984), 155–168.

Chapter 2

1. Ann Evory, ed. *Contemporary Authors* (Detroit: Gale Research Co., 1979), 374.
2. *Language Arts,* March 1979, 290.

Chapter 3

1. Norma Klein, "The Pleasures of Midlist," *Publisher's Weekly,* 28 March 1986, 58.
2. Evory, ed. *Contemporary Authors,* 374.
3. *Publisher's Weekly,* 2 September 1983, 81.
4. Charlotte W. Draper, *Horn Book,* February 1984, 62.
5. Anne Connor, *School Library Journal,* November 1983, 94.
6. Phy interview.

Chapter 4

1. Lois A. Strell, *School Library Journal,* October 1983, 180.
2. Kevin Kenny, *VOYA,* October 1983, 203.
3. *Publisher's Weekly,* 27 August 1979, 838.

4. Joyce Smothers, *Library Journal,* 15 February 1981, 470.
5. Peter Steuwe, *Quill and Quire,* October 1981, 44.

Chapter 5

1. *Publisher's Weekly,* 9 October 1978, 64.

Chapter 6

1. Letty Cottin Pogrebin, "A Young Indian and a New Father: 'Mom, the Wolf Man and Me,'" *New York Times Book Review,* 24 September 1972, 8.
2. Marilyn R. Singer, *School Library Journal,* December 1972, 60–61.
3. Alice Bach, *New York Times Review,* 29 September 1974, 8.
4. Ibid.
5. C. N. Wooldridge, *School Library Journal,* October 1980, 156.

Chapter 7

1. Elizabeth D. and Ben F. Nelms, "Not All Hearts and Flowers," *English Journal,* February 1985, 98–103.
2. Denise L. Moll, *School Library Journal,* May 1984, 90; Sari Feldman, *VOYA,* February 1985, 327.

Chapter 8

1. Roger Sutton, "The Critical Myth: Realistic YA Novels," *School Library Journal,* November 1982, 33–35.

Chapter 9

1. Klein, "The Pleasures of Midlist," 28.
2. *Publisher's Weekly,* 7 October 1974, 55.
3. Barbara Koenig Quart, *Nation,* 11 June 1983, 738.

Chapter 10

1. Evory, ed., *Contemporary Authors,* 374.
2. Phy interview.

3. Ibid.

4. Julius Lester, "The Kind of Books We Give Children: Whose Nonsense?" *Publisher's Weekly,* 23 February 1970, 86–88.

Selected Bibliography

PRIMARY SOURCES

1. Novels for Adults

American Dreams. New York: E. P. Dutton, 1987.
Coming to Life. New York: Simon & Schuster, 1974.
Girls Turn Wives. New York: Simon & Schuster, 1976.
Give Me One Good Reason. New York: G. P. Putnam's Sons, 1973.
Lovers. New York: Viking Press, 1984.
Wives and Other Women. New York: St. Martin's Press, 1982.

2. Short Story Collections for Adults

Love and Other Euphemisms. New York: G. P. Putnam's Sons, 1972.
Sextet in A Minor. New York: St. Martin's Press, 1983.

3. Novels for Young Adults

Angel Face. New York: Dial Press, 1984.
Beginner's Love. New York: E. P. Dutton, 1983.
Bizou. New York: Viking Press, 1983.
Breaking Up. New York: Pantheon, 1980.
The Cheerleader. New York: Alfred A. Knopf, 1985.
Domestic Arrangements. New York: M. Evans & Co., 1981.
Family Secrets. New York: Dial Press, 1985.
Give and Take. New York: Viking Press, 1985.
Going Backwards. New York: Scholastic, 1986.
Hiding. New York: Four Winds, 1976.
It's Not What You Expect. New York: Pantheon, 1973.
It's OK if You Don't Love Me. New York: Dial Press, 1977.

Love is One of the Choices. New York: Dial Press, 1978.
Older Men. New York: Dial Press, 1987.
The Queen of the What Ifs. Greenwich: Fawcett Publications, 1982.
Snapshots. New York: Dial Press, 1984.
The Swap. New York: St. Martin's Press, 1983.
Taking Sides. New York: Pantheon, 1974.

4. Books for Children

Baryshnikov's Nutcracker. New York: G. P. Putnam's Sons, 1983.
Blue Trees, Red Sky. New York: Pantheon, 1975.
Confessions of an Only Child. New York: Pantheon, 1973.
Dinosaur's Housewarming Party. New York: Crown Publishers, 1974.
Girls Can Be Anything. New York: E. P. Dutton & Co., 1973.
A Honey of a Chimp. New York: Pantheon, 1980.
If I Had My Way. New York: Pantheon, 1974.
Mom, the Wolf Man and Me. New York: Pantheon, 1972.
Naomi in the Middle. New York: Dial Press, 1974.
Robbie and the Leap Year Blues. New York: Dial Press, 1981.
Tomboy. New York: Four Winds, 1978.
A Train for Jane. New York: Feminist Press, 1974.
Visiting Pamela. New York: Dial Press, 1979.
What It's All About. New York: Dial Press, 1975.

5. Novelizations (novels based on screenplays)

French Postcards. Greenwich: Fawcett Publications, 1979.
Sunshine. New York: Holt, Rinehart & Winston, 1975.
Sunshine Christmas. New York: Dell Publishing Co., 1977.
The Sunshine Years. New York: Dell Publishing Co., 1975.

6. Interviews

Allene Stuart Phy interview with Norma Klein, Lilburn, Georgia, 11 April 1986.
Mark West interview with Norma Klein, New York City, 11 June 1985. Portions of this interview were published in *New York Times Book Review*, 24 August 1986, 20.

7. Articles

In *Something about the Author,* edited by Anne Commire, 7:152–54. Detroit: Gale Research Co., 1975.
"Growing Up Human: The Case for Sexuality in Children's Books," *Children's Literature in Education 8* (Summer 1977):80–84.
"My Say," *Publisher's Weekly,* 9 March 1984, 106.
"The Pleasures of Midlist," *Publisher's Weekly,* 28 March 1986, 58.
In *Something about the Author,* Autobiography Series, edited by Adele Sarkissian, 1:155–68. Detroit: Gale Research Co., 1984.

SECONDARY SOURCES

1. Books

Broderick, Dorothy M. *Image of the Black in Children's Fiction.* New York: R. R. Bowker Co., 1973.
Bryfonski, Dedria, ed. *Contemporary Literary Criticism,* 12:296–303. Detroit: Gale Research Co., 1980.
Carlsen, G. Robert. *Books and the Teenage Reader.* Rev. ed. New York: Harper & Row, 1971.
Evory, Ann, ed. *Contemporary Authors,* vols. 41–44, 374. Detroit: Gale Research Co., 1979.
Nilsen, Alleen Pace, and Donnelson, Kenneth L. *Literature for Today's Young Adults.* 2d ed. Glenview: Scott, Foresman & Co., 1985.
Riley, Carolyn, ed. *Children's Literature Review,* 2:97–101. Detroit: Gale Research Co., 1976.
Stine, Jean C., and Marowski, Daniel G., eds. *Contemporary Literary Criticism,* 30:235–44. Detroit: Gale Research Co., 1984.
Sutherland, Zena. *The Best in Children's Books 1966–1972.* Chicago: University of Chicago Press, 1973.

2. Articles

Abrahamson, Jane. "Still Playing It Safe: Restricted Realism in Teen Novels." *School Library Journal,* May 1976, 38–39.
Decter, M. "Judy Blume's Children." *Commentary,* March 1980, 65–67.
Engdahl, Sylvia. "Do Teenage Novels Fill a Need?" *English Journal,* February 1975, 48–52.
Hanckel, Frances, and Cunningham, John. "Can Young Gays Find Happiness in YA Books?" *Wilson Library Bulletin,* March 1976, 528–34.

Lester, Julius. "The Kind of Books We Give Children: Whose Nonsense?" *Publisher's Weekly,* 23 February 1970, 86–88.

Nelms, Elizabeth D. and Ben F. "Not All Hearts and Flowers." *English Journal,* February 1985, 98–103.

Neufeld, John. "The Thought Not Necessarily the Deed: Sex in Some of Today's Juvenile Novels." *Wilson Library Bulletin,* October 1971, 147–52.

Root, Shelton L. "The New Realism, Some Personal Reflections." *Language Arts,* January 1977, 10–24.

Stanek, Lou Willett. "The Junior Novel: A Stylistic Study." *Elementary English,* October 1974, 947–53.

Stanek, Lou Willett. "The Maturation of the Junior Novel: From Gestation to the Pill." *School Library Journal,* December 1972, 34–39.

Sutton, Roger. "The Critical Myth: Realistic YA Novels." *School Library Journal,* November 1982, 33–35.

3. Selected Book Reviews

American Dreams
Mithers, Carol Lynn. *New York Times Book Review,* 29 March 1987, 23.

Angel Face
Feldman, Sari. *VOYA,* February 1985, 327.
Goodman, M. *Interracial Books for Children Bulletin,* January 1984, 33.
Mall, Denise L. *School Library Journal,* May 1984, 90.
Shreve, Susan Richards. *New York Times Book Review,* 17 June 1984, 24.

Beginner's Love
Kenny, Kevin. *VOYA,* October 1983, 203.
Perez-Stable, Maria A. *Library Journal,* 15 April 1983, 840.
Strell, Lois A. *School Library Journal,* October 1983, 180.

Bizou
Connor, Anne. *School Library Journal,* November 1983, 94.
Draper, Charlotte W. *Horn Book,* February 1984, 62.
Publisher's Weekly, 2 September 1983, 81.
Wilms, Denise M. *Booklist,* 15 October 1983, 360.

Blue Trees, Red Sky
Bradley, Lynn. *School Library Journal,* November 1975, 64.
Elleman, Barbara. *Booklist,* 1 December 1975, 516.

Breaking Up
Bagnall, Norma. *ALAN Review,* Spring 1981, 13.
Meryl, Jay. *Interracial Books for Children Bulletin,* no. 3, 1981, 19.
Pearson, Sheila. *VOYA,* June 1981, 28.
Wooldridge, C. N. *School Library Journal,* October 1980, 156.

The Cheerleader
Andrews, Deborah. *School Library Journal,* November 1985, 98.
Chamberlin, Leslie. *VOYA,* April 1986, 31.

Coming to Life
Publisher's Weekly, 7 October 1974, 55.

Confessions of an Only Child
Burton, Gabrielle. "Book World." *Washington Post,* 19 May 1974, 3.
Kirkus Reviews, 1 February 1974, 110.
Langton, Jane. *New York Times Book Review,* 5 May 1974, 16.

Domestic Arrangements
Hollander, Deborah, and Miller, L.E., *VOYA,* October 1981, 34.
Rolnick, Amy. *School Library Journal,* August 1981, 82.
Smothers, Joyce. *Library Journal,* 15 February 1981, 470.
Stuewe, Paul. *Quill and Quire,* October 1981, 44.

French Postcards
Booklist, 15 December 1979, 595.
Publisher's Weekly, 27 August 1979, 383.
Smothers, Joyce. *Library Journal,* 15 October 1979, 2236–37.
Todisco, Paula. *School Library Journal,* November 1979, 96–97.

Girls Can Be Anything
Stavn, Dione Gersoni. *School Library Journal,* May 1973, 64.
Sutherland, Zena. *Bulletin of the Center for Children's Books,* April 1973, 126.

Girls Turn Wives
Ferrari, Margaret Burns. *America,* 10 July 1976, 18.
Pollitt, Katha. *New York Times Book Review.* 25 April 1976, 49.

Give Me One Good Reason
Kennedy, Eileen. *Best Sellers,* 15 November 1973, 376–77.
Rosenthal, Lucy. "A Singular Parent," *Ms.,* January 1974, 36–37.

Going Backwards
Campbell, Patricia J. *New York Times Book Review,* 15 March 1987, 29.
Eaglen, Audrey B. *School Library Journal,* January 1987, 83–84.

Hiding
C. B. J. *Kliatt Young Adult Paperback Book Guide,* Winter 1978, 9.
Flowers, Ann A. *Horn Book,* December 1976, 629–30.
Willison, Marilyn. *West Coast Review of Books,* March 1977, 58.

A Honey of a Chimp
Babbitt, Natalie. *New York Times Book Review,* 13 July 1980, 22.
Harrington, Pat. *School Library Journal,* April 1980, 112.

If I Had My Way
Kirkus Reviews, 1 February 1974, 106.
Kuskin, Karla. *New York Times Book Review,* 5 May 1974, 47.
Sutherland, Zena. *Bulletin of the Center for Children's Books,* September
    1974, 11.

It's Not What You Expect
Balducci, Carolyn. *New York Times Book Review,* 3 June 1973, 8–10.
Savage, Lois E. *Best Sellers,* 15 May 1973, 98.
Booklist, 15 September 1973, 122.
Kirkus Reviews, 15 February 1973, 194.
Sutherland, Zena. *Bulletin of the Center for Children's Books,* July-
    August 1973, 172.

It's OK if You Don't Love Me
Schene, Carol. *School Library Journal,* May 1977, 83.
Wakefield, Dan. "Firepersons and Other Characters," *New York Times
    Book Review,* 1 May 1977, 10.

Love and Other Euphemisms
Bryan, C. D. B. *New York Times Book Review,* 15 October 1972, 31–33.

Love Is One of the Choices
Campbell, Patricia J. *Wilson Library Bulletin,* April 1979, 579.
Johnson, Nora. "Love and Madness," *New York Times Book Review,* 25
    March 1979, 28.
Smothers, Joyce. *Library Journal,* 15 November 1978, 2351.
Publisher's Weekly, 9 October 1978, 64.

Mom, the Wolf Man and Me
Booklist. 1 January 1973, 449–50.
Fisher, Margery. "Mom, the Wolf Man, and Me." In *Who's Who in Children's Books: A Treasury of Familiar Characters of Childhood.* (New York: Holt, Rinehart & Winston, 1975), 54.
Heins, Ethel L. *Horn Book,* February 1973, 57.
Kirkus Reviews, 1 September 1972, 1027.
Pogrebin, Letty Cottin. "A Young Indian and a New Father: 'Mom, the Wolf Man, and Me.' " *New York Times Book Review,* 24 September 1972, 8.
Singer, Marilyn R. *School Library Journal,* December 1972, 60–61.

Naomi in the Middle
Kirkus Reviews, 1 November 1974, 1151.
Sutherland, Zena. *Bulletin of the Center of Children's Books,* March 1975, 116.
Yolen, Jane. *New York Times Book Review,* 3 November 1974, 48.

Older Men
White, Liffy K. *School Library Journal,* April 1987, 111–12.

The Queen of the What Ifs
Hartos, Marsha. *School Library Journal,* April 1983, 125.
Zvirin, Stephanie. *Booklist,* 15 June 1982, 1364.

Sextet in A Minor
Hooper, William Bradley. *Booklist,* 15 February 1983, 763.
Publisher's Weekly, 24 December 1982, 47–48.
Quart, Barbara Koenig. *Nation,* 11 June 1983, 738.

Snapshots
Noah, Carolyn. *School Library Journal,* December 1984, 90.
Davidson, Andrea. *VOYA,* April 1985, 49.

Sunshine
Nilsen, Alleen; Tyler, Karen B.; and Kozarek, Linda. "Reluctantly Yours, Books to Tempt the Hesitant." *English Journal,* May 1976, 90–93.

The Sunshine Years
Strickland, Margaret. *School Library Journal,* April 1976, 90.

The Swap
Donavin, Denise P. *Booklist,* August 1983, 1448.
Publisher's Weekly, 29 June 1984, 103.

Taking Sides
Bach, Alice. *New York Times Book Review,* 29 September 1974, 8.
Booklist, 15 July 1974, 1254.
Coyle, Cathy S. *School Library Journal,* October 1974, 119.
Kirkus Reviews, 1 July 1974, 688.
Sutherland, Zena. *Bulletin of the Center for Children's Books,* November
    1974, 45.

Tomboy
Language Arts, March 1979, 290.

What It's All About
DJB. *Language Arts,* May 1976, 519.
Hearne, Betsy. *Booklist,* 1 November 1975, 369.
Nelson, Alix. *New York Times Book Review,* 16 November 1975, 50.
Shapiro, Leila C. *School Library Journal,* November 1975, 79.

Wives and Other Women
Lockhart, Marilyn. *Library Journal,* 1 June 1982, 1112.
Publisher's Weekly, 7 May 1982, 73.
Simson, Eve. *Best Sellers,* September 1982, 218.

Index

About the Author

Allene Stuart Phy has taught in Africa and has worked as a Peace Corps consultant for programs in language and literature for Zaire, Kenya, and Liberia. She has followed postdoctoral studies at universities in four foreign countries and conducted travel seminars to Italy and the Soviet Union. For several years she taught courses in history of religions, comparative literature, and children's literature at George Peabody College, Vanderbilt University. She developed and taught a class in literature for exceptional children. The author of many articles and translations, she has also been a staff book reviewer for *School Library Journal, Fantasy Review*, the *Nashville Tennessean*, and the Montgomery *Journal-Advertiser*. Her books include *The Bible and Popular Culture in America* and *Mary Shelley*. Currently Professor of English at Alabama State University, Phy continues to work with elementary and high school educators. She recently designed and taught a seminar in oriental literature and culture for secondary teachers. With her husband, Professor Frederick B. Olsen, she also works on programs to improve writing skills and the teaching of the humanities in Alabama and the nation.